Louis Braille
A TOUCH OF GENIUS

By C. Michael Mellor

NATIONAL BRAILLE PRESS ✌ BOSTON

In memory of my mother and father
— C. M. M.

NATIONAL BRAILLE PRESS
88 Saint Stephen Street
Boston, MA 02115-4302
www.braille.com

First published in the United States of America by National Braille Press Inc.
William M. Raeder, President

Library of Congress Cataloging-in-Publication Data

Mellor, C. Michael.
  Louis Braille : a touch of genius / By C. Michael Mellor.
    p. cm.
  Includes bibliographical references and index.
  ISBN 0-939173-70-0 (alk. paper)
  1. Braille, Louis, 1809-1852—Juvenile literature. 2. Blind teachers—France—Biography—Juvenile literature. I. Title.
  HV1624.B65M45 2006
  686.2'82092—dc22

                               2005029150

Book design by Judith Krimski, Krimski Design, Inc.

Manufactured in the United States of America
Henry N. Sawyer Company, Inc., Charlestown, Massachusetts
10 9 8 7 6 5 4 3 2 1

NATIONAL
BRAILLE
PRESS

TABLE OF CONTENTS

A TOUCH OF GENIUS

LA JEUNE AVEUGLE DU PONT NEUF.

For the braille edition of this book, all pictures have been described by experts skilled in the art, for example:

Girl on Bridge: Early-19th-century color lithograph. In dusky evening light, a girl with eyelids lowered kneels upon a layer of straw beside the stone wall of a bridge. In her right hand she holds out a metal cup by the handle. In the other, she grasps the narrow end of a white, cone-shaped paper lantern. Its radiant light illuminates her thin, heart-shaped face and diminutive mouth drawn in a warm smile. Brown hair falls in curls around her face from beneath a gray scarf tied in folds on her head. A narrow cord winds loosely around her wrist and is attached to both the handle of the cup and the collar of a sleeping black dog, right, snuggled against her knees. A straight stick is tucked into the bend of her right elbow. She wears a golden-brown shawl over a dress and white apron. A scarf around her neck is pleated behind a cloth sign fastened across her chest on which French words are written by hand, "Aux Ames Sensibles," which translates "To the Kind-Hearted."

Below the picture, curved lines frame and embellish the title, "La Jeune Aveugle du Pont Neuf," which translates "The Blind Girl of the Pont Neuf (New Bridge)."

Louis Braille
TOUCH OF GENIUS PRIZE
FOR INNOVATION

"To give blind people the ability to write, to allow them to surmount this obstacle
that so markedly restricts their social relations… is a subject that should have been
proposed for a prize by the various betterment societies."
～ Louis Braille ～

National Braille Press is proud to announce the
Louis Braille Touch of Genius Prize for Innovation
to be granted to an individual or group
who advances the cause of literacy
for blind and deafblind people worldwide.

For more information, please visit
www.braille.com

Leading support for this book and for the Louis Braille Touch of Genius Prize for Innovation from

❧

THE GIBNEY FAMILY FOUNDATION

Additional funds graciously given by

❧

E. MATILDA ZIEGLER FOUNDATION FOR THE BLIND

The author wishes to thank the many fine people who gave so generously of their time and talent to bring Louis Braille to life:

A special thanks to Diane Croft for her invaluable editorial vision.

Isabelle Balot (*French*)
Cathy Bickerdike (*stamps*)
Martine Bruel (*letter translations*)
Valerie Ching (*picture descriptions for braille edition*)
Daniel Cuff (*researcher*)
Andrea Doane (*picture descriptions for braille edition*)
Joan Giurdanella (*letter translations*)
Sandra Goroff (*book publicity*)
Tony Grima (*marketing*)
John Hernandez (*researcher*)
Melissa Hirshson (*braille transcription*)
Tanya Holton (*fundraising*)
Angela Kessler (*final proof*)
Paula Kimbrough (*researcher*)
Judith Krimski (*book designer*)
Jefferson Lyons (*braille production*)
Terry McAweeney (*project consultant*)
Martha Parravano (*copyeditor*)
Nicholas Racheotes (*historical reviewer*)
Jonathan Sawyer (*printer*)
Helen Selsdon (*researcher*)
Ken and Gunilla Stuckey (*stamps & reviewers*)
Jan Seymour-Ford (*researcher*)
Marianne Wojnar (*business plan*)

Merci Beaucoup

Our profound gratitude to our esteemed colleagues in France
without whom this book would not be possible.

Notre profonde gratitude tient à signaler l'aide inestimable
de nos collègues françaises sans lesquelles ce livre n'aurait jamais vu le jour.

Margaret Calvarin

Directrice

Maison Natale de Louis Braille

Zoubeïda Moulfi

Chargée d'études Documentaires

Institut National des Jeunes Aveugles (INJA)

Noëlle Roy

Conservateur

Musée "Valentin Haüy"

Zina Weygand

Chercheur en Histoire

Laboratoire Brigitte Frybourg pour

L'Insertion Sociale des Personnes Handicapées

Conservatoire National des Arts et Métiers

This book began in a most improbable manner. In 1995, a fax arrived at the *Matilda Ziegler Magazine for the Blind* in New York City, where I was the editor, inviting me to attend a conference in Copenhagen on "the blind in history." My academic background in history, plus two decades of working in the field of blindness, compelled me to go. The conference was everything it was billed to be in "wonderful, wonderful" Copenhagen.

The "Second International Conference on the Blind in History," in 1998, was a smashing success. The most moving aspect was walking in the footsteps of Louis Braille, exploring the modest house in Coupvray where he was born, seeing a reconstruction of the very workshop where he pierced his eye with a sharp tool belonging to his harness-maker father, entering the room at the Institut National des Jeunes Aveugles (INJA) in which Braille taught music and in whose infirmary he died.

Just around the block from INJA, we visited the outstanding museum of the Association Valentin Haüy, founder of the first school for blind children in Europe. There, we examined cleverly made apparatus from many parts of the world that enabled blind people to acquire skills they would otherwise, unthinkingly, have been denied. Beyond all this treasure, what brought me literally to a stop was seeing, at INJA, a collection of letters actually written in Louis Braille's own hand. Braille's voice, so to speak, could at last be heard, rather than that of others writing about him. Instantly I resolved to obtain permission to have the letters translated into English and published.

As soon as I returned to New York I set my course, completely unaware that INJA itself was planning to publish a facsimile of the letters. They appeared in 1999 in a beautifully produced limited edition of 200 copies, *Louis Braille 1809-1852 Correspondence*. Nonetheless, the trustees and M. Gerard Gonzales, director of INJA, graciously granted me permission to translate the letters into English. And so I embarked on my little pamphlet.

But it was not to be. During a casual conversation with my friend Diane Croft, vice president for publishing at National Braille Press in Boston, Massachusetts, I mentioned that I was working on a translation of Louis Braille's letters. She at once insisted that National Braille Press publish them — what publisher would be more appropriate? I readily agreed, and we both eventually spent a week in Paris, exploring the project in more depth. I had already found that there were other letters. But on this trip we found information that had never appeared in English, and also obtained permission from Margaret Calvarin, curator of La Maison Natale de Louis Braille (Louis Braille Museum), to use many of the beautiful photographs in her collection. So, largely by chance, my little pamphlet transmogrified into this book.

At a time when the preferred form of biography seems to be what has justly been called "pathography" — emphasizing the weaknesses, flaws, offensive prejudices, and bad behavior of the subject — this glimpse offers no such revelations. It is true that, at least in the English-speaking world, Louis Braille has been sentimentalized as a poor blind boy who lived a saintly life at a school for the blind, invented a reading and writing system that now bears his name, and then died at an absurdly young age. This portrayal is not entirely untrue. But by allowing Louis Braille to speak for himself through his letters and other writing — by examining in more detail the often unhealthy environment in which he performed his pioneering work, the awful sadness he faced, and his chronic poor health, but also his friendships, his extraordinary musical talent, his doggedness in the face of prejudice against his code, even traces of wry humor — then we will at last have had a glimpse of the real man.

— **C.M.M., Brooklyn, New York**

Peint par Roehn.   Tiré du Cabinet de Mr de Cypierre.   Lithographié par Melle Hubert.

L'AVEUGLE ET LE TILBURY.

Translation of Letters

Of the twenty-four extant letters housed at the Institut National des Jeunes Aveugles (INJA) in Paris, ten were written by Louis's own hand, eight were dictated to sighted writers, four were written on a device that Braille helped to invent called a raphigraphe (basically a dot-matrix printer), and two were composed by, and in the handwriting of, Braille's brother, Louis-Simon.

Letters written in Louis's own handwriting presented few problems, even though there are no capital letters and little punctuation. His grammar is excellent, but sometimes he seems to forget what he has just written and repeats a word or phrase, making the meaning less clear. Deciphering his meaning was the task faced by myself and two fine translators, Joan Giurdanella and Martine Bruel.

The letters Louis wrote on a raphigraphe are perfectly legible to this day. In fact, Louis helped to invent this method of printing so that people who are blind could, for the first time, write to people with eyesight.

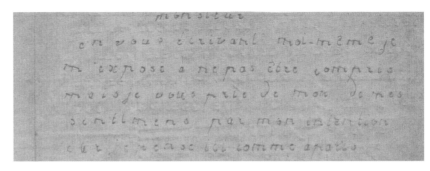

Louis's own handwriting.

One of Louis's raphigraphe letters.

The letters dictated to sighted writers were the most difficult to translate. Even if the handwriting could be made out, and in most letters this was not easy to do, the scribes were scarcely literate and simply wrote down the sounds they heard — or thought they heard. Words were run together, so that what looked like one word might well represent two or more words.

Three stages were required to translate these letters: first, the handwriting had to be deciphered — what letters of the alphabet did those unruly squiggles represent? Then came the task of figuring out what French words those words stood for, and finally, the translation into English.

Here is an example:

Transcription: "Mademoiselle votre seur soufter toujour de ses dans…"

French: "Mademoiselle votre soeur souffre toujours de ses dents…"

English: "Mademoiselle your sister always suffers with her teeth…"

A letter dictated by Louis to a barely literate scribe.

Minature on ivory by Lucienne Filippi

"When the body sinks into death, the essence of man is revealed."

Antoine de Saint-Exupéry

PROLOGUE

Midday on January 6, 1852, Louis Braille received the last rites and gently embraced his brother, Louis-Simon, and several close friends for the last time. Even when he could no longer speak, he moved his lips with "tender movements that spoke from the heart more than words could."[1] Everyone in the room was weeping.

Around four in the afternoon the death agony began, and at seven thirty, on the evening of Epiphany, the twelfth day of Christmas, "Louis Braille entrusted his soul to the hands of God."[2] The infirmary at the residential school in Paris where he died was turned into a sanctuary, where friends and students came to pray and cry over the loss of their respected teacher and cherished friend. Virtually unknown outside Paris, Braille had just turned 43.

The Institut National des Jeunes Aveugles (National Institute for Blind Youth) in Paris, France. This beautiful structure, built in 1843, is still in use. Louis Braille lived and worked here as a teacher from the time it opened until his death nine years later.

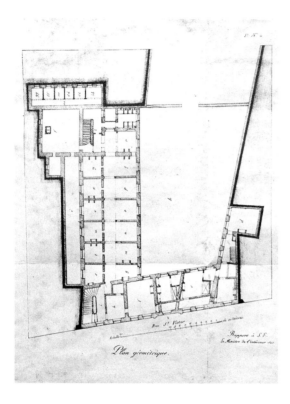

Above and facing page:
The original school that Louis Braille attended,
the Royal Institution for Blind Youth, was
located near the river Seine on rue Saint-Victor,
one of the least healthy sections of Paris.
The Institution was damp, unsanitary, and
dangerous to the health of the children and
teachers. It was here that Louis Braille invented
the code that made it possible for blind people to
read and write with ease.

THE FINAL DAYS

The chronic illness that took his life was tuberculosis, a prevalent malady at the time. Louis was probably infected by it at the notoriously unhealthy residential school for the blind on rue Saint-Victor in Paris, where Braille had studied and taught for twenty-four years. By the time the school moved to a newly built facility in 1843, his health had been completely undermined.

In early December 1851, Louis Braille had been admitted to the infirmary of the Institut National des Jeunes Aveugles, where "a violent bleeding spell almost took his life and he developed the most frightening symptoms."[3] Braille felt himself near death and sent for the priest, who solemnly administered the sacraments. Yet, the next day Braille felt somewhat better and told his friend Hippolyte Coltat, "Yesterday was one of the most beautiful and greatest days of my life. When you have experienced that, you understand all the majesty and power of religion…. I have tasted the supreme delights… I am convinced that my mission on earth has been accomplished…. It is true, I asked God to carry me away from the world — but I felt I did not ask very strongly."[4]

Ten days later, Christmas arrived and Louis Braille observed it from his bed. He asked a close friend to offer some inspiring thoughts pertinent to the season and his illness, but he warned him to be brief and to the point. Braille disliked wordiness in pious sentiments as much as he did in ordinary speech. When distraught family and friends encouraged him to hope for a cure, he answered simply, "You know I do not pay in that coin; you do not have to dissimulate with me."[5] Sensing the end was drawing near, he called in a lawyer to draw up his will — a document that reflects the generosity and selflessness that characterized his life.

LAST WILL AND TESTAMENT

Hippolyte Coltat, a former student and close friend who stayed with Braille during his final days, left a written account saying, "Braille prepared for death with the same sangfroid (self-possession) he would have shown in preparing for a short trip."[6] First of all, he forgave all debts. By living within his modest income, Braille could afford to be generous to others, often lending money to those in need and keeping an accurate accounting of it. He had a good head for business, wisely managed his property in Coupvray, and supplemented his teacher's salary by playing the organ in churches around Paris. There was time to call in his debts before he died, but Braille chose instead to forget them.

Façade méridionale, et principale entrée rue St Victor.

Echelle de 20 Mètres

Next he took care of his family, making sure that his mother, Monique, would receive an annuity for life. (His father had died in 1831, when Louis was 22, and his sister Marie-Céline Marniesse died ten years later in 1841.) He left other securities to his goddaughter and niece, Louise-Céline Marniesse, and his nephew, Louis-Théodore Carron. Braille never married and left no children, but his letters bespeak a great affection for his niece and nephew.

Paris, 5 August 1848

My dear nephew,
I deeply regret not being able to accept your wedding invitation but be certain that, in spite of having to stay in Paris for my affairs, my spirit and my heart will be with you at the town hall and at the church of Mespuis, with my fervent and affectionate wishes for your own happiness and for the highly estimable person who chose to unite in marriage her own destiny to yours.

I am certain that you will always grace the two respectable families to which you both belong. Your union will delight your parents and the many friends who like me regret not being with you on that solemn day, but we shall make up for it when you visit Paris, Chessy, or Coupvray. I shall add that if you linger too long, I shall come to Milly.

So, my dear friends, take heart and join your fates under the protection of religion and you will attain great happiness, and will deserve the esteem of good people, the devotion of your friends, the affection of your relatives — mine in particular — and especially the love of my good and respectable mother who so much looks forward to holding in her arms her dear new granddaughter Clémence.

I beg you to embrace your parents for me and to convey my respectful greetings to Mr. and Mrs. Bertheaux whom I shall be very happy to meet someday soon, and for you, my dear nephew and very dear niece, many embraces from the heart,

Your completely devoted uncle,
Louis Braille

To his friend Coltat, Braille left his savings account, piano, moveable furniture, books, linen, scientific instruments, and "in general all I own at the Institute." It is significant that he left behind scientific instruments. We can only speculate as to what they were and how he used them. Alexandre-René Pignier, the head of the institute when Braille was a student and teacher there, remarked that Louis was talented in many areas but was "particularly disposed toward science."[7]

As he did in life, Braille took care to acknowledge those kind people who had helped him in many small ways: the boy

Facing page:
Throughout his life, there remained a strong emotional bond between Louis Braille and his native village of Coupvray. It was here at the Church of St-Pierre (St. Peter's Church) that he was baptized on January 8, 1809, and here that his body was laid to rest in the village cemetery — about 100 yards from the church.

4

CHARITIES LOUIS BRAILLE SUPPORTED
(BEQUESTS FROM HIS WILL)

BRAILLE'S SAVINGS ACCOUNT OF 918 FRANCS (300 FRANCS WAS EQUIVALENT TO ONE HUNDRED DAYS' WORK FOR A LABORER) WAS REDUCED TO 585 FRANCS AFTER EXPENSES. THE SALE OF HIS PIANO, WHICH HE HAD ACTUALLY BEQUEATHED TO COLTAT, RAISED THE BALANCE AGAIN, BUT PAYMENT OF A FEW REMAINING BILLS LEFT ONLY 780 FRANCS FOR DISTRIBUTION TO VARIOUS CHARITIES ACCORDING TO LOUIS BRAILLE'S WISHES — AN AMOUNT FAR LESS THAN HE HAD HOPED TO GIVE.

✧

Braille left the largest bequest to the Institut National des Jeunes Aveugles (National Institute for Blind Youth) to help graduates find jobs. Braille had hoped to leave four or five hundred francs for this purpose, but the sum had to be reduced to 292 francs.

✧

The second largest bequest went to the Society for the Care and Aid of Blind Workers[8] in France, a group that assisted blind individuals to become self-supporting, and on whose committee Braille had served.

✧

A devout Roman Catholic, Braille supported the Work for the Propagation of the Faith.

✧

Another sum of money was bequeathed to Mademoiselle Champion of Metz to continue her work supplying embossed books.

✧

Smaller bequests went to the Infirmary of Marie-Thérèse to say masses for the repose of Braille's soul, and to the curé of Coupvray for masses and for "a remembrance to the church of my village."

LE JEUNE AVEUGLE

Louis Braille walked with a confident gait and was usually guided by a sighted boy, such as the one shown here guiding a blind man. In a gesture that typified his appreciation of the help he received in his life, Braille bequeathed 40 francs to the boy who acted as his sighted guide.

who acted as his sighted guide, another boy who worked in the infirmary, and the night watchman. Many of his belongings were divided up as souvenirs among relatives, colleagues, former students, and friends. Everyone knew that this was what he would have liked.

Found among his belongings was a small wooden box on which was written, "To be burned without opening."[9] But the box was opened before it was burned and was said to contain IOUs. This is curious, since in his will he had forgiven all debts. Perhaps he had prepared the box long before his final illness to ensure that those who owed him money would be relieved of their obligations after he died. Did the box also contain letters from Pignier or other papers, perhaps in braille? We shall never know.

BRAILLE'S FACE

Even though at his death Louis Braille was not famous — only a few friends and colleagues recognized his achievements — Pierre-Armand Dufau, director of the Institute at the time, had the foresight to have a plaster cast ("death mask") made

of Louis Braille's face for the purpose of sculpting a bust. François Jouffroy, a renowned Parisian sculptor and teacher at the Ecole des Beaux Arts, did the work from a block of marble provided by the Interior Minister.[10] (The original death mask has disappeared.) Given that Dufau had initially opposed Braille's new code, perhaps he was making amends.

Coltat tells us that "his friends had his portrait made, examples of which were multiplied by a marvelous art — as a gesture of friendship." Most likely he was referring to a daguerreotype, a new photographic process named after one of its inventors, Louis Jacques Mandé Daguerre, a Parisian artist and contemporary of Braille's. The original daguerreotype has also been lost, but an engraving based on it was used to make this image — the only "photographic" likeness we have of Louis Braille's face.

His delicate facial features show the sunken cheeks of a man who had endured chronic illness, but who nonetheless retained a pleasing appearance. He was slim, fair skinned, blue-eyed (his right eye was opaque, but streaks of blue could be seen in the partly opaque left eye), and had curly blond hair. His friend Hippolyte Coltat records that an "agreeable smile" often illuminated the face of Louis Braille — a smile that his chronic illness could not erase.[11]

LAID TO REST

Monique Braille understandably wanted her son buried in his native town. A funeral service was held on January 8, 1852, at the Institute in Paris. The next day, Louis-Simon arranged for a black cart to carry Louis's body back to Coupvray, where it was interred in the plot that already held his father and sister.

Something dramatic happened in the Braille family soon after Louis was buried. Hippolyte Coltat wrote the following letter to Braille's brother, Louis-Simon, with veiled references to "false allegations." It is not unusual for family disagreements to break out after a death, and the Braille family was like any other. The language hints at financial mismanagement, but there are no clues as to why there was discord — perhaps some decision made by Louis-Simon had upset them. Coltat obviously felt so strongly about it that he wrote a letter imploring him to take care of himself.

Paris, 30 January 1852

My good Mr. Braille,
We are really worried about the state of your health, please drop us a line so we can set our minds at rest. I beg you, don't let yourself become upset by your family's bad judgment. Let your conscience be your guide, which should be enough for you. You also have the testimony of all your good deceased brother's

This image of Louis Braille was derived from a daguerreotype, taken shortly after his death. This is the visage of a dead man; in life, he kept his eyes open. "Louis was of medium height, slender, quite streamlined and elegantly muscular. His head leaned forward, his blond hair curled naturally, his movements were free and easy." [12]

friends. We are all thoroughly convinced of the falseness of the allegations that are aimed at you. Let all that be trampled underfoot, and think only about taking care of yourself and getting better. I advise you also not to postpone writing to me.

Your very devoted,
H. Coltat

BRAILLE'S HANDS

Louis Braille's remains lay undisturbed in the Coupvray cemetery for one hundred years. At the time of his death, the braille code he had invented more than twenty-five years earlier had yet to be recognized in France as the official method for reading and writing among blind people. Official recognition came in 1854, two years after his death. On the centennial of his death, the French authorities decided that his achievements were so outstanding that Louis Braille merited a place in the Pantheon, alongside the most distinguished men and women in French history. His remains were disinterred in 1952 and transferred to Paris after a devotional service in St. Peter's Church in Coupvray.

His native village was reluctant to let him go; they insisted that some token of their homegrown genius remain in Coupvray. A compromise was struck: Louis Braille's hands would remain in Coupvray. Those hands that had imparted to the hands of blind people a perfected means of reading and writing are preserved in a marble container that sits on top of his grave.

On June 20, 1952, one hundred years after his death, Louis Braille's remains were disinterred and transferred from the cemetery in Coupvray to the Pantheon in Paris. The bones of his hands, however, were kept in an urn in the cemetery of his native village.

1. - COUPVRAY. - Monument de Braille. - *Lehoux Ed.*

Coupvray locals pose in front of Louis Braille's monument, erected near Town Hall.

Louis Braille's grave in Coupvray, France, where he was originally interred. His hands ("the most precious relics") are entombed in a small container that sits on top of his gravestone.

LA COMMUNE DE COUPVRAY GARDE PIEUSEMENT DANS CETTE URNE LES MAINS DU GENIAL INVENTEUR.

IN THIS URN, THE TOWN OF COUPVRAY PIOUSLY KEEPS THE HANDS OF THE GENIUS INVENTOR.

The coffin of Louis Braille in St. Peter's Church in Coupvray before being transferred on June 22, 1952, to the Pantheon in Paris.

COMMEMORATIONS IN PARIS

There was no mention of Louis Braille's death in the Paris newspapers of 1852. One hundred years later dignitaries from all over the world converged on Paris to pay belated homage to their genius inventor, among them the deaf and blind Helen Keller. She gave a speech in what the *New York Times* reported as "faultlessly grammatical" French. To a rousing ovation from the hundreds of other braille readers in attendance, she declared, "...we, the blind, are as indebted to Louis Braille as mankind is to Gutenberg."[13]

As the coffin was borne through the streets of Paris towards the Pantheon, hundreds of white canes tapped along behind, in what the *Times* called "a strange, heroic procession."[14]

Helen Keller's hands move gracefully across a page of braille.

Louis Braille's home.

HOME

In the first few weeks of 1809, three baby boys were born who changed the course of history: Abraham Lincoln, sixteenth President of the United States; Charles Darwin, British father of the theory of evolution; and Louis Braille, the French inventor of a means of literacy for blind people worldwide. Unlike Lincoln and Darwin, Braille's genius is little known outside his native land, except among those who have been touched by his gift of literacy.

Louis was a small, listless baby, too sickly even to suck milk from his mother's breast. He was registered with the town authorities the next day and baptized three days later for fear he might die.[1] Disease struck hard in early-19th-century France, and infant mortality was high, even for the wealthy. Still, under the devoted care of his mother and family, Louis grew more robust. Mother and father were thrilled with their new baby, who came along, perhaps unexpectedly, when Simon-René was 44 and Monique 39. Simon-René proudly announced that Louis would be his "companion in old age." The doting parents called him their little "Benjamin" — a reference to the beloved son of the biblical Jacob — and he became their favorite.

FAMILY LIFE

Simon-René supported his family as a harness maker (*bourrelier*), a trade first practiced by his own father some sixty years earlier. In an agrarian society, a *bourrelier* was a man of some stature, well known to the farming community and frequently visited by neighboring farmers over the course of a year.[2] He made the leather tack — collars, straps, bridles — that allowed a farmer to tap and control the strength of a horse, the chief source of power on a farm and one of the few means of transport until well into the

Louis Braille's father made the equipment that harnessed and controlled the strength of a horse. Not merely practical, his highly decorative harnesses were also works of beauty. As a boy, Louis Braille helped his father make the colored fringes for the harnesses.

A FAVORITE SON

Louis Braille was born in the little town of Coupvray, 25 miles east of Paris, on January 4, 1809. He was the last child of Simon-René Braille and his wife of 17 years, Monique (née Baron). They already had three children: Monique-Catherine-Joséphine, born 1793; Louis-Simon, born 1795; and Marie-Céline, born 1797. Louis was the youngest by twelve years.

2 - COUPVRAY (S.-et-M.) — Lavoir des Médisances   Edit.

"Lavoir des Médisances" (the Gossips' Wash House), dating back to the Middle Ages, incidentally functioned as a socially important communications center. This is where the women socialized us they did the laundry, exchanged gossip, and found out what was going on around town and elsewhere.

19th century. Simon-René was adept at his trade, earning the title of master harness maker before he was 27. "It was a point of honor with the master to deliver only work well done, to strive for perfection in the whole and in every detail."[3] Young Louis was to draw on these traits — attention to detail and a desire for perfection — to invent a means of literacy for people around the world.

Life for Monique Braille, a wife and mother in rural France at the turn of the 19th century, was arduous. Lacking today's labor-saving amenities, Monique spent most of her waking hours taking care of the children, preparing food, cleaning, sewing, spinning, washing and mending clothes, and helping on the farm. There were chickens and a cow to attend to, and in the fall, she and the children helped to make hay as winter fodder.[4] Monique and Simon-René always encouraged young Louis to join in the work. Over the years, the industrious and frugal Braille family acquired an additional seven and a half acres of land, and managed their own two and a half acre vineyard, which yielded a year's supply of wine, stored in huge casks in the cellar.

Even with today's medical advances, it is unlikely that Louis's wounded eye could have been saved, but the healthy (left) eye might have been treated with corticosteroids and immunosuppressive drugs. The development of pathology in a healthy eye after the other eye has been injured was noticed as long ago as AD 1000,[5] though no term existed for this phenomenon until 1830, when William Mackenzie, a leading Scottish ophthalmologist of his time, devised the term "sympathetic ophthalmia."[6] This is now thought to be an auto-immune disease in which the mechanism the body uses to repair damage goes awry and attacks healthy tissues. The seemingly drastic measure of surgically removing Louis Braille's injured eye within two weeks of injury might have prevented the development of blinding inflammation in his healthy eye.[7]

"The Accident," a drawing by André Harfort, depicts an inquisitive and energetic three-year-old boy climbing up to reach one of his father's sharp leather-working tools. This dramatic rendering is more fanciful than factual.

CALAMITY IN THE WORKSHOP

How young Louis Braille injured his eye in his father's workshop one summer day in 1812 is not clear. The most reliable account comes from Hippolyte Coltat, a former schoolmate and close friend of Louis's:

"One day, at the age of three, sitting beside his father, who was working and lovingly thinking about his little Benjamin, the boy wanted to work too, and imitate the movements he saw his father make. In one of his little hands he seized a leather strap, and in the other a serpette (a slender, curved knife rather like a small pruning hook) and there he was at work. Weakness often invites trouble; and it did: The sharp tool veered out of control at an angle and stabbed the poor worker in the eye."[8]

Medical knowledge at that time could not save the eyesight of their Benjamin. Lily water, thought to possess healing powers, was applied by an old woman from the village, probably doing more harm than good to the injured right eye. Louis's other (left) eye became inflamed, and the sight in that eye was eventually lost, too. The right cornea became totally opaque, and the left eye partially so, with blue "striations."[9] His eyes would have been very painful during this period; he would have cried a lot and needed much mothering. It is not known how long the process continued, but by age five, two years after the accident, Louis was completely blind.

Left: Louis Braille was born in this modest farmhouse built in the 18th century. At one time, the Braille property consisted of several stone buildings on both sides of the street, but only the family home has been restored as a museum.

MAISON NATALE DE LOUIS BRAILLE

Louis Braille's family home in Coupvray has been converted into a museum open to the public.[10] The World Blind Union (WBU) entered into a partnership with the Commune of Coupvray in 1957 to ensure the upkeep and future of "this most important shrine in the world for blind people."[11] The museum is located on the outskirts of Paris, near EuroDisney, and is easily accessible by road or train (see page 115 for more information).

Below: La Maison Natale de Louis Braille contains many artifacts and mementoes from his life, including this set of dominoes that looks very much like the six-dot matrix he used for his code.

A Guided Tour of the Braille Home

A frequent visitor to Louis Braille's birthplace is Euclid J. Herie, a leader in the field of blindness and an avid braille reader.[12] His evocative description speaks of the deep feelings blind people have for the man who bequeathed them the gift of literacy.

"I have come to Coupvray, France, to visit and to restore myself at La Maison Natale de Louis Braille, the birthplace of Louis Braille. This is a place of pilgrimage for those without sight who seek liberation through literacy. On this fine May morning, I am sitting on a simple bench in the back garden awaiting the arrival of Mme. Calvarin, the curator of this magical and beloved place. The birds sing, and a gentle breeze is blowing. The air is redolent of fresh hay, roses, lilacs, and the bright orange poppies that grow along the hedgerows and in the fields...."

Above: Family life revolved around this cozy kitchen/living room. Here, meals were prepared and eaten by the entire family, who would indulge in laughter and horseplay.

Right: In this wood-fired oven, Monique Braille baked bread and pies. A recess next to the oven provided warmth for processing the Brie cheese characteristic of that region of France.

"The two days I am here are hot sleepy days — only the odd other visitor. I have been given full access to the house, which is very cool, thanks to the thick stone walls. The lovely oak-beamed room where Louis Braille was born — *la salle commune* is the room where all the important activities of family life would take place — the conception and birth of the four Braille children in the beautiful

18

oak framed alcove bed; the family meals prepared with the use of a wood burning bread oven and eaten at the rectangular oak table in the centre of the room; a cheese recess next to the oven which provided sufficient warmth for the making of Brie cheese. The room would have been heated by the large fireplace; washing done in the stone sink — a large flat stone from which the water drained away through the wall into the backyard. The room has a simple cozy charm that belies all that would have happened here — cooking smells, family work and family play, conversation and learning. Today it is peaceful, but the room resonates with the life that once inhabited it.

"The workshop of Simon-René Braille, although a reconstruction of the original, is, without a doubt, the most important room in this house for those of us who are blind. Were it not for the tragedy that cost Louis Braille his sight at the age of three, blind people may not have found the liberation we sought. It is difficult to imagine what genius, if any, would have invented a way for blind people to read and write. For it was Braille's loss of sight, caused in his father's workshop, which provided him with the inspiration to create the braille system.

"To give readers a sense of the power present even today in this small room, I would like to quote from Dr. Kenneth Jernigan[13] who wrote these words following a visit in 1995:

'The spirit of the place moved me as I sat in a chair with a leather strap seat in the saddle shop and felt the worn surface. I looked at the tools of the harness-maker's trade and held in my hands a sharp tool of the type that blinded Louis Braille in that very room at that very bench....

'The visit to Louis Braille's home and the reading of his letters caused me to wonder what he thought as he was growing up and how he felt, but it also caused me to think about my own childhood and how I felt and thought. It strengthened my determination to do all I can to preserve and continue the Louis Braille heritage, for except for him I might still be living as a virtual prisoner on the farm where I grew up in Tennessee, hungering to know and longing for freedom. Instead, I escaped to a broader world of books and achievement, to a life of opportunity and hope, and to a distant day in France when I stood at the birthplace of my benefactor and reached across the years to a common bond.'"[14]

A corner of Simon-René's workshop, where he skillfully plied his trade as a harness maker. Here you see a well-worn workbench and chair with its seat of crossed leathern thongs.

Coupvray vineyard.

COUPVRAY

The people of rural Coupvray embraced their native son without reservation following his accident and throughout his life. Although Braille was destined to move beyond his local village — even into the higher echelons of Parisian society — it was to Coupvray that he returned time and again to renew his spirits on the family farm and in the surrounding woodlands. Louis never lost his love of the tranquility and simple pleasures of the countryside: "My dear mother, I am getting bored in the big city and I'll be happy to breathe the fresh air of the countryside, to walk with you through the vines. I am afraid they may not be ripening quickly, but if the warm weather comes back the grapes will improve and I will too." [1]

The character of Coupvray has been preserved through the centuries: the tiled roofs, the farmyards, gardens and orchards, the village shops and town cemetery. All around is open country.

LA FIN D'UNE TRISTE JOURNÉE.

(Le Parjure.)

The end of a sad day.

Understandably, Simon-René and Monique were devastated that their "Benjamin" could no longer see, and tormented, no doubt, by thoughts that they could have prevented the accident if only they had supervised their inquisitive son more closely. The Braille family would have known nothing about raising a blind child, and whatever they knew about blindness could not have been encouraging. Devout Roman Catholics, Monique and Simon-René were exposed to Biblical teachings that viewed blindness as a curse or even a punishment. In St. John's Gospel (9:1-4), when Christ encounters a man who had been blind since birth, his disciples ask him, "Rabbi, for whose sin — for his own or his parents — was he born blind?" Jesus responded, "It was not that this man sinned or his parents, but that the works of God might be made manifest in him." (Most people remember the question but not Jesus' surprising answer.) The devil himself was referred to as "the prince of darkness." The Talmud included a command that, upon approaching a blind person, one must pronounce the same benediction that was customary on the death of a close relative.[2]

Most blind people during Louis Braille's lifetime lived lives of utter destitution; only those who were supported by

Wille Del.t et Sculp.t

Picquet Jeune, Scripsit.

a well-situated family or patron managed reasonably well. Those living in rural areas worked in gardening or fruit picking, or as peddlers or beggars who roamed the country. Blind people who lived near cities worked as musicians, town criers, bell ringers, water carriers, or circus performers, but most lived near the edge as beggars or even prostitutes. Some blind people actually preferred to be beggars because of the freedom it entailed: they were answerable to no one. There were instances where blind beggars who had learned a trade in a school nevertheless returned to their mendicant ways, refusing to take up employment in a workshop.

There were at least two other blind men in Coupvray around Louis Braille's time. An 1831 report to the Sous-Préfet of Coupvray lists, along with Louis Braille, a 66-year-old man who became blind as an adult from a "paralysis." He had been a day laborer, husband, and father of several children before he went blind, but was now destitute.

In this humorous drawing, two blind men, far from the city, approach each other in hopes of a handout.

The other blind man listed was a 49-year-old bachelor who gradually became blind for no apparent reason, and could no longer earn enough to meet his needs.[3]

Fortunately, Simon-René and Monique were down-to-earth people. Trusting their instincts, they decided that Louis would receive an education and that he would be encouraged to participate in the normal activities of family life. Their little boy was not going to be like those "unfortunate beings who sit and wile [sic] their long life of night away within doors, unseen and unknown by the world."[4] It helped that the Braille family was literate — a rarity among villagers at that time. A friend of the Braille family later reported that Louis learned the alphabet at an early age, at home, by feeling the shapes of letters made with upholstery nails that had been hammered into a wooden board.[5]

CONSEQUENCES OF WAR

France, at the time of Louis Braille's birth, was at the peak of its power. Napoleon Bonaparte had won successive victories over such great nations as Austria, Prussia, and Russia. Paris was no longer convulsed by a revolutionary violence, as it had been in the 1790s, but had become the capital of a vast empire that encompassed Western Europe.

Remote though Coupvray was from the commotion in Paris, it could not escape the terrible consequences of Napoleon's constant war with the rest of Europe. Several times the town was overrun by armies — both Napoleon's and those of his opponents to the east. In January 1814, Napoleon's retreating armies made huge demands on all peasants in the region for grain and animals. After the national army departed, the Russians, en route to Paris, entered town a month later, and they too lived off the farmers.

Between March and June of 1815, Napoleon returned to lead France until his ultimate defeat near Waterloo. For the next three years, France was occupied by a multi-national army to ensure compliance with the terms of the Vienna peace settlement. Thus, the nation of Braille's childhood was a defeated, humiliated one. For several months, the Braille household was required to billet Prussian soldiers. Billeting of soldiers required more than simply tolerating unruly houseguests. Soldiers were inclined to demand the best rooms, eat the best food, drink all the wine, and sometimes even burn the furniture and hit defenseless women and children.[6] It must have been distressing for the whole family, but especially for young Louis, to live with the intrusion of strangers, eating and sleeping in close

quarters and speaking in foreign tongues.

Poverty struck Coupvray hard in 1816 — the year without a summer.[7] A poor harvest coupled with the exactions of the military caused hunger throughout the land and made people susceptible to disease. A smallpox epidemic ravaged Coupvray that same year. Smallpox — a disfiguring, often fatal, disease, accounting for one-in-three deaths among children — was the leading cause of blindness at the turn of the century. (Fortunately, although Simon-René refused to have his family vaccinated,[8] no one in the Braille household became infected.)

THE PARISH PRIEST

As war continued to rain misery on the village of Coupvray, St. Peter's Church had to find a new priest when Abbé Pillon, who had baptized Louis Braille, died early in 1815.[9] Father Jacques Palluy, a learned man and former Benedictine monk, was discovered to be eminently qualified. In such a small, close-knit community, Father Palluy came to know the Braille family well. He could tell that young Louis was intelligent and full of curiosity about the world he could no longer see. In the peace and quiet of the old presbytery, near St. Peter's Church, or outdoors under the trees on warm days, Abbé Palluy began to teach a boy who was eager to learn.[10] Part of his education included a strong Christian belief in love, kindness, and humility — attributes that became deeply engrained in Louis Braille's character.

After a year of private tutoring, Father Palluy, like Louis's parents, realized that Louis's blindness was no barrier to acquiring an education. In 1816, when the town appointed a new teacher, Antoine Bécheret, Palluy approached him with a most unusual request: Would the young teacher accept the seven-year-old Louis as a student in the village school? Bécheret agreed. For the next two years, a boy who lived nearby came to the Braille home and took Louis by the hand, and together they walked up the steep road to school. Louis was the only blind child in the class, and one of the brightest. His superior intelligence was detected almost immediately by Bécheret: "The child dumbfounded him with his responses by turns pertinent and amusing."[11]

Alas, this promising arrangement was short-lived. In the aftermath of the French Revolution many traditional practices were dismantled with little thought for unintended consequences. Trouble began in 1818, when the school was forced to adopt a new teaching system called "mutual instruction," where students taught one another under the supervision of a teacher. Bécheret told the mayor that he would not adopt it; in his opinion, it reduced the role of the teacher and could not be carried out during the summer months when so many children left school to help with the harvest. Threatened with the loss of his job if he did not cooperate, Bécheret unwillingly complied with the new teaching method and was sent to the School of Mutual Instruction in Melun for training.

Abbé Palluy was equally alarmed by these revolutionary changes and declared the school not only anti-Christian but a sham (comédie).[12] Several students left at the end of the year to attend schools where traditional practices were still intact, and Palluy sought a similar situation for Louis. Bécheret had heard of a boarding school in Paris

This list of students enrolled in the public school in Coupvray (23 November 1818) shows that Louis Braille attended school with his niece, Josephine Céline Carron.

that accepted blind children, gave them an education, and taught them various trades to help them become self-sufficient. Palluy approached the lord of the manor in Coupvray, the Marquis d'Orvilliers, for his help in securing a place for Louis.

Fortuitously, d'Orvilliers was already somewhat familiar with the school. On December 26, 1786, he had been present at Versailles when Valentin Haüy, the school's founder and a pioneer in the education of the blind, had arranged for his students to demonstrate their newly acquired skills before King Louis XVI and his court. M. d'Orvilliers had been so impressed with Haüy's teaching innovations that he had funded several of Haüy's benevolent projects.[13] He agreed to write to the school director, requesting Louis's admittance.[14] It is doubtful that Louis would have been accepted without this connection.

IN LOUIS'S BEST INTEREST

When Simon-René and Monique were told that a school for the blind existed in Paris, at first they were not sure it was suitable for Louis. To send their favorite child so far away — twenty-five miles was four hours by stagecoach — to the imposing, noisy, and noisome capital must have been a heart-breaking proposition for them both. Their eldest son and daughter had already married, and their younger daughter, Marie-Céline, was to be wed in June. With Louis's departure, the nest would be empty.

Eventually they were persuaded that it would be in Louis's best interest to attend the school. On February 15, 1819, having just reached the age of ten, Louis boarded a stagecoach for Paris with his father.

This journey marked the end of Louis's secure childhood. Raised in a loving and attentive family in a small town where the Brailles were well known and respected, Louis Braille showed enormous fortitude in leaving home. Such inner strength was not surprising: at a young age, Louis had seen war, famine, disease — endured even the loss of his eyesight. He must have been aware, if not consciously, that to be alive was to be vulnerable. But Louis also knew that he could rely on his family. These firm roots were a source of strength and renewal that he would draw on throughout his short life.

This letter Louis wrote to his mother from the school in Paris shows a yearning to be near family and old friends, even as an adult.

Coupvray woodlands.

26

Paris, 10 September 1847

My dear mother,

I am planning to come and spend next week with you; I plan to arrive in Chessy Monday night, but if the weather turns out bad I shall delay my arrival in spite of my great desire to see you. I am getting bored in the big city and I'll be happy to breathe the fresh air of the countryside, to walk with you through the vines. I am afraid they may not be ripening quickly, but if the warm weather comes back, the grapes will improve and I will too.

I am delighted to think that I will be back with my family of which I have seen only you and my brother since last year. So I will be happy to see my sisters Josephine and Virginia[15] again, their children, the Marniesse[16] family, and, above all, my goddaughter who should be well behaved since she has just made her First Communion. I am not forgetting the people who have honored me with their friendship.

I hope the weather will be good so that we can visit little Vincent, whom I promised to visit before he left. We have a lot of visits to make, but I am distressed when I think about having to return to Paris the following Saturday, but I will come back a week later and I hope to play the game of Boston[17] with the excellent Mrs. Raymond whose respectable family has given me such pleasant moments.

Accept, my dear Mother, the renewed affection of your respectful son.
L. Braille

A well just outside the Braille house was the family's only source of fresh water. Two hundred years later, it still contains water.

Coupvray. (S.-et-M.). — La Statue de Braille.

The townsfolk of Coupvray embraced Louis.

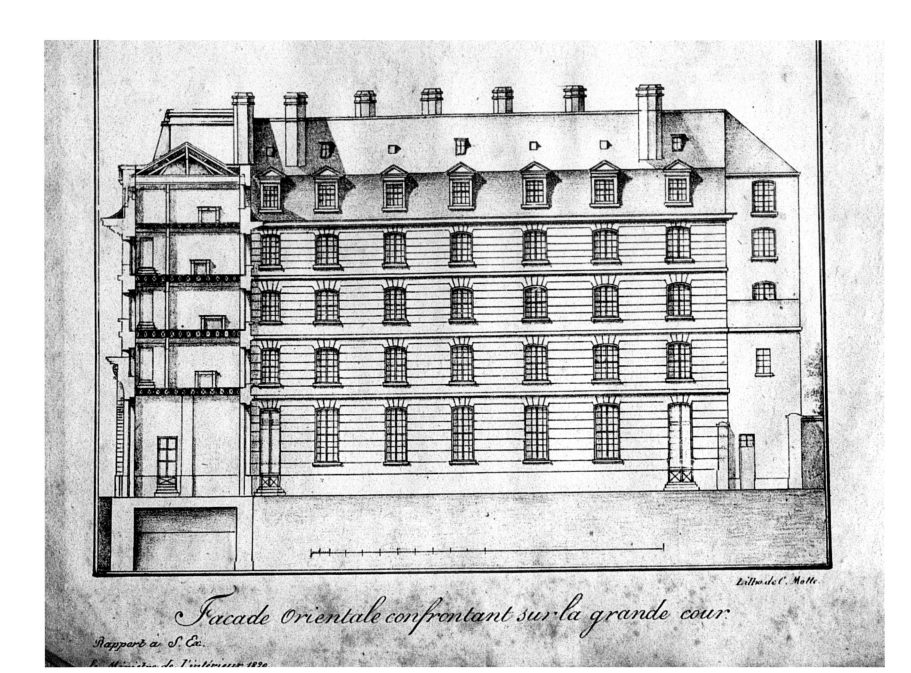

Façade Orientale confrontant sur la grande cour.

Rapport à S. Ex.

le Ministre de l'intérieur 1830.

28

VALENTIN HAÜY

When the stagecoach carrying Louis Braille and his father pulled up at the Institution Royale des Jeunes Aveugles on February 15, 1819,[1] the master craftsman must have been appalled at the dilapidated condition of the school. Most of the building, a former seminary and temporary prison during the revolution,[2] was more than 200 years old. Inside were narrow, winding stairs — one for boys and one for girls, to ensure segregation of the sexes. For students who had to use their hands to guide themselves, the clammy walls and rickety staircases were a "challenge hurled at the blindness of the children."[3] The school piped in filthy, untreated water from the nearby Seine for cooking and washing, just two hogsheads per day (at most, 280 gallons) and hardly adequate for up to 90 students plus 15 employees.[4] The children were allowed one bath per month.[5] Still, the Paris school was far better than anything previously available to blind children born into modest circumstances.

Facing page:
The decrepit building that housed the school had been used as a prison for refractory priests during the revolution. In September 1792, following the overthrow of the monarchy, prisoners were thrown from the 4th floor windows to their deaths.

Flyer distributed at the Saint Ovide Fair.
This humiliating display of blind musicians
made the young Valentin Haüy determined
to improve the lives of blind people.

HAÜY'S EPIPHANY

The education that Louis Braille received at the Institution would have been unthinkable but for the enthusiasm, dedication, courage, and foresight of one man, Valentin Haüy. His determination to educate blind children was sparked as a young man, when he witnessed a degrading spectacle at the popular street fair of Saint Ovide in 1771.[6] There, an "orchestra" made up of nine blind men from the Quinze-Vingts, a residence for blind people founded by Saint Louis around 1260,[7] entertained a crowd of people out for a good time.

Tricked out in long red robes, and wearing pointed dunce caps and opaque glasses, the ensemble played horribly discordant "music." Seated on a peacock throne, the "conductor," wearing wooden clogs and a hat with ass's ears, tried unsuccessfully to keep time.[8] The crowd laughed uproariously at this bizarre performance, which was a great money maker for the owner of the café where it was staged.

The 26-year-old Haüy was not amused. "A very different sentiment possessed our soul," he said later, "and we conceived, at that very instant, the possibility of realizing, to the advantage of these unfortunate people, the means of which they had only an apparent and ridiculous enjoyment: The blind, said we to ourselves, do they not know objects by the diversity of their shapes? Are they mistaken in the value of a coin? Why could they not distinguish a *C* from a *G* in music, or an *a* from an *f* in spelling if their characters were rendered plain?"[9]

INTERPRETER TO THE KING

Born November 13th, 1745, into a hard-working family of weavers from Saint-Just-en-Chaussée in Picardy, Haüy had a tenacious temperament that proved essential in the years ahead when he was ridiculed for his belief that blind people could be educated. Haüy made his living as an interpreter, eventually acquiring the honorary title "interpreter to the king," which surely helped him drum up business. He was indeed a clever man: he could work in 10 languages, though most of his business consisted of translating commercial and legal documents, and was adept at deciphering codes — a skill always in demand. Haüy's fascination with language might well account for his unusual interest in teaching blind youngsters to read and write.

AGE OF ENLIGHTENMENT

Haüy's disgust at the St. Ovide spectacle arose in part from his Christian background, which inculcated sympathy for suffering humanity (his brother was a priest).[10] His thinking also reflected new attitudes toward the human condition embraced by some educated people during a period called the Enlightenment — basically "a loose, informal, wholly unorganized coalition of cultural critics, religious skeptics, and political reformers from Edinburgh to Naples, Paris to Berlin, Boston to Philadelphia."[11]

Such thinkers rejected the idea that fate or God determined the condition of human beings. They believed instead that human suffering could be alleviated if reason were applied to solving social, political, cultural, economic, and technical or scientific problems. Claims of authority from either throne or altar must never be allowed to interfere with free enquiry.[12]

Valentin Haüy (right), founder of the first school for the blind in Europe, and his famous priest-scientist brother, Abbé René-Just, a founder of the science of mineralogy.

DENIS DIDEROT (1713–1784)

One of the most original and influential figures of the French Enlightenment was the essayist, polymath, and philosopher Denis Diderot, whose *Encyclopédie* became an important organ of educated opinion in pre-Revolutionary France and elsewhere. Published under constant threat of government censorship and withdrawal of the license to publish, the *Encyclopédie* took twenty-one years to complete, from 1751 to 1772. Diderot assembled an impressive group of writers, scientists, and priests to write articles for a project that eventually took the form of 35 volumes (12 of which were illustrations).

Earlier, in 1749, Diderot published his *Lettre sur les aveugles à la usage de ceux qui voient* (Letter on the Blind for the Use of Those Who See), mainly to display his qualifications to be editor of the proposed *Encyclopédie*.[13] It landed him in jail.[14] What shocked conventional thinkers was Diderot's statement that the famous blind mathematician, Nicholas Saunderson, (see sidebar) had claimed he would believe in God only if he could touch Him.[15] Diderot seemed to be denying the existence of God, and for that, he had to pay the price.

One of the most accomplished blind individuals of the 18th century was Nicholas Saunderson, Lucasian Professor of Mathematics at the University of Cambridge in England. Born in Yorkshire in 1682, he became totally blind as an infant when smallpox destroyed his eyeballs.[16]

His mathematical genius became apparent at an early age, but conventional education at a private academy did not suit him, and he soon left. Instead, he studied in his own way, using only a good author and someone to read to him. "By the strength of his own Genius he could easily master any Difficulty that occurred therein."[17] Too poor to be formally admitted, he was allowed to study at Christ's College, Cambridge, where he was treated with great respect and given lodgings and free access to the library. He was such an outstanding teacher that he could scarcely find time to accommodate all those who sought instruction. When the highly prestigious position of Lucasian Professor of Mathematics became vacant, Saunderson was the best-qualified person — his candidacy was endorsed by none other than Sir Isaac Newton.[18] Since he lacked the requisite degree, Queen Anne ordered that he be awarded an L.L.D., "Doctor of Letters." His inaugural speech "was delivered from memory, in Latin with such just Elocution, and in a manner so graceful as to gain him the universal Applause of his Audience."[19]

Professor Saunderson was more than a calculating machine. He enjoyed many hobbies, including horseback riding, hunting, and poetry. He played the flute like a master. After several years of suffering from scurvy, which caused numbness in his limbs and made one foot gangrenous, he died in 1739. As the end drew nigh, Saunderson gave his wife, Abigail, and their two children his blessing: "I wish you all happiness; live virtuously, and learn in me to die quietly." He then asked them to leave the room,

"their lamentations being more uneasy to him than the approach of death."[20]

Engrav'd for ÿ Universal Magazine, for J. Hinton in Newgate Street.

NICHOLAS SAUNDERSON, L.L.D.
late Lucasian Proffessor of Mathematics in Cambridge.

BLIND MAN OF PUISEAUX

Haüy was familiar with Diderot's *Lettre* (see sidebar) and had probably also read Diderot's two-page article on the blind, *Aveugles*, published some two decades earlier in the first volume of the *Encyclopédie*.

From Haüy's point of view, the chief interest of Diderot's *Lettre* lay in his descriptions of the competence of blind individuals. Diderot had visited a blind man in Puiseaux (whose name we are never told) and was astonished at the man's capacious and accurate memory and stubborn independence. Born blind into a prosperous family, he depleted his fortune during a brawling, riotous youth. Eventually, he settled down, married, and had a sighted son whom he taught to read by means of letters of the alphabet in relief. This blind man earned his keep by making liqueurs to pique refined Parisian palates.

The blind man of Puiseaux could thread a needle and do pretty pieces of needlework. His musical aptitude was such that he could perform a piece after being told only the notes and their values. Asked whether he would like to have eyesight, the confident man remarked that, but for his curiosity about the nature of eyesight, he would just as soon have longer arms. "[T]he eye sooner ceases to see than the hand to touch, that to improve the organ I have would be as good as to give me that which is wanting in me."[21]

Haüy later said that Diderot's description of the blind man from Puiseaux teaching his sighted son to read, and of Nicholas Saunderson teaching mathematics to a circle of sighted men, emboldened him to dare to teach blind people to read and write.[22]

A MUSICAL SENSATION

A woman who greatly inspired Haüy's mission was Maria Theresia von Paradis, a celebrated young musician from Vienna (see sidebar). Accompanied by her devoted mother, she spent six months in Paris as part of a European concert tour, creating a sensation wherever she performed. One man reported, "The talent of Mademoiselle von Paradis on the harpsichord, despite her total blindness, is the most astonishing thing in the world."[23]

An offer to demonstrate her skills and the adaptive equipment she used appeared in the *Journal de Paris*, April 24, 1784,[24] and Haüy seized this opportunity to visit von Paradis at her lodgings. There, he learned that she could both read and write using a portable press that pricked letters onto a sheet of paper. This ingenious device had been made for her by fellow Austrian Wolfgang von Kempelen, a skilled mechanic who had taught her to read by means of cutout cardboard letters.[25] A letter she had written by this means

Early attempts were made to reproduce illustrations and maps in relief, like this Leaning Tower of Pisa from a much later period.

"was full of the most delicate sentiments," Haüy said.[26]

During her music tour, Maria von Paradis also met Ludwig Weissenbourg, an educated blind man from Mannheim with whom she had previously exchanged letters. Music was a common interest, for he was an accomplished flautist. He supplied her with a board for doing math, tactually identifiable playing cards, and maps in relief. These maps were a feat of human ingenuity, using beads of different sizes and glazed sand to mark geographic features.[27]

MARIA THERESIA VON PARADIS
(1759-1824)

The cause of Maria Theresia von Paradis's blindness is a mystery. It was described as "convulsive twitching" in her eyes at the age of three.[29] The famous, soon to be notorious, Viennese pioneer of hypnosis, Fredrich Anton Mesmer (1734-1815), claimed he could cure her, but she became very nervous under his treatments and eventually returned to her parents' home. Whatever the facts, she remained blind.

Her inborn musical skill would probably not have flourished if she had not had access to the best teachers because of her social connections. Her father was the godson of Empress Maria-Theresa, who was also the mother of Marie-Antoinette, Queen of France. The Empress granted von Paradis a stipend to help her obtain an excellent musical and general education.

Through her personal example, von Paradis convinced influential people throughout Europe that blind people could use their sense of touch to acquire an education. In later years she devoted herself to composition and teaching, especially encouraging young female musicians. Her music is still performed.[30]

VALENTIN HAÜY

RADIOU DE LA TRONCHERE STATUE
Léon Gaucherel sculpt

Paul Bucquet dir.   Imp. Salmon, Paris.

Well aware that Maria von Paradis enjoyed advantages unavailable to most people, Haüy was nevertheless convinced that it would be feasible for less-exalted blind people to master the specialized techniques she and others used: "The aim we had before us was the following: to rescue the blind from the distressing and even dangerous burden which idleness creates; to help them find a means of livelihood in pleasant and easy tasks; to integrate them into society; to comfort them in their misfortune...."[28] With this in mind, he set out to develop the means to educate poor blind children.

This statue of Valentin Haüy with his first student, François Le Sueur, a 17-year-old blind beggar, stands in the forecourt of the Institut National des Jeunes Aveugles in Paris. In 1784, Haüy agreed to pay the boy what he would have earned from begging if he would become his student.

THE FIRST STUDENT

More than ten years passed before Haüy was able to put his theories into practice. In 1784, he was introduced to François Le Sueur, a blind teenager who helped to support his impoverished family by begging near churches. Whenever the youth received a coin from a passerby, he scurried away to share it with his three sisters and two brothers, the youngest still being suckled by their mother.[31] Le Sueur had become blind from "convulsions" when just six weeks old. Determined not to be a burden on his family, he took to begging as soon as he was old enough.

In late adolescence, he sought a better life and, on his own initiative, contacted the Philanthropic Society,[32] an organization that assisted young blind people from poor families. Unfortunately, at age 17, he was just over the age limit set by the Society to qualify for a pension. But all was not lost. By great good fortune, Haüy had just a few months earlier presented to the Society his plan for educating blind people. An anonymous Society official, identified only as a "generous friend of mankind," remembered Haüy's presentation and offered Le Sueur the opportunity to participate in this plan.[33]

Haüy gladly took on this highly intelligent youth, even though his family complained that Haüy's proposal would deprive them of an indispensable source of income.[34] Far from wealthy, and with a wife and two children to support, Haüy nevertheless agreed to pay François as much as he would have made by begging, if he would take lessons. Thus began, in June 1784, a most unusual tutorial arrangement: the teacher paying the student!

Progress was swift, even though both participants were making it up as they went along. By means of wooden letters, François quickly learned the alphabet. Soon there was another breakthrough. One day, while casually running a finger over a printed funeral notice, Le Sueur asked if the shape he could feel was a letter "o." Indeed it was. The pressure of the printing press had left an indentation in the paper that sensitive fingers could identify. Haüy then deliberately embossed letters of the alphabet into several sheets of paper and found that Le Sueur was capable of recognizing the different letters. After three months of practice, he could both read and write.[35]

Late that fall, Haüy and his first student demonstrated their joint achievement

FRANÇOIS LE SUEUR, *Aveugle,* *âgé de 18 ans, Lisant à l'aide des Doigts &c.*

SOUS-INSTITUTEUR DES ENFANS-AVEUGLES

Secouru par la SOCIÉTÉ PHILANTROPIQUE

François Le Sueur, a blind illiterate beggar when Valentin Haüy began to teach him, learned to read and write in three months. To his right is a case of type used to print pages readable by touch; at his left is a small printing press. Behind him is an embossed music score meant to be read tactually, but not really practical. The globe and maps, including one of South America hanging on the wall, attest to his knowledge of geography.

before a distinguished gathering at the Academic Bureau of Writing. Haüy first read a "Memoir on the education of the blind," and then a nervous Le Sueur demonstrated his skill at reading with his fingers. Among the texts he read were excerpts from the life of Nicholas Saunderson, a distinguished blind mathematician. In a process resembling typesetting, Le Sueur "wrote" phrases dictated to him and performed mathematical calculations.[36]

One month later, on December 22, 1784, Haüy and Le Sueur gave another demonstration, this time at the Royal Academy of Sciences. This meeting got off to a bad start. When asked to read a passage of embossed text selected by a member of the audience, Le Sueur could not make it out. Haüy stopped the demonstration after only three words, saying that the young man was having trouble. Soon Le Sueur was back on track, blushing with pleasure when the audience applauded his success.[37] Similar exercises were given before other organizations, and each time a collection was taken up to benefit the Philanthropic Society.[38]

FOR CHILDREN BORN BLIND

Haüy now felt confident enough to open a small school in his apartment on rue Coquillière. Twelve students, all poor children receiving stipends from the Philanthropic Society, were chosen as most likely to benefit from Haüy's new teaching methods. The Society also paid Le Sueur to teach other blind students the skills he himself had so recently acquired. As the number of students grew, more space was needed, and once again the Philanthropic Society lived up to its name, renting space in 1786 for the embryonic Institution at 18 rue Notre-Dame-des-Victoires. This may be regarded as the official opening of l'Institution des Enfants Aveugles (Institution for Children Born Blind), the first educational establishment for the blind in Europe.

Haüy aimed to give his students instruction in three areas: a broad general education that included reading, writing, arithmetic, history and geography; music; and manual skills that might help them to pay their way in the world. A free thinker, Haüy advanced the idea that a general education should be available to girls as well as boys.

BOOKS FOR THE BLIND

The school had been functioning only a short time when Haüy published his *Essai sur l'éducation des aveugles* (Essay on the Education of the Blind) in 1786.[39] By then, Haüy had accomplished much. He had above all devised a way to fabricate books in embossed type that could be read by the fingers. No one before Haüy had ever tried seriously to make printing available to ordinary blind people, or had established collections of books printed in relief. Three-and-a-half centuries had elapsed after Gutenberg's innovation of printing before the same benefit was offered to blind people.

Breaking new ground, Haüy had to solve all manner of technical problems. First, typefaces used for printing ordinary books were of no help because they are cast in metal as a mirror image, and composed in a line of type set from right to left. Embossing raised letters, on the other hand, requires "right-reading." During "printing," strong, dampened paper is pressed hard against the metal type, which indents the paper to yield an impression of print in relief. Haüy, therefore, had to arrange for type founders to prepare the dies and matrices from which to cast right-reading type. This was an expensive business, carried out under the auspices of the Philanthropic Society and paid for by the financier M. Rouillé de l'Etang.[40]

Many modifications were made to the printing press so that it would produce enough pressure to impress the shape of the type on paper. Likewise, it was necessary to find paper that could be dampened yet would not tear under pressure. How damp should the paper

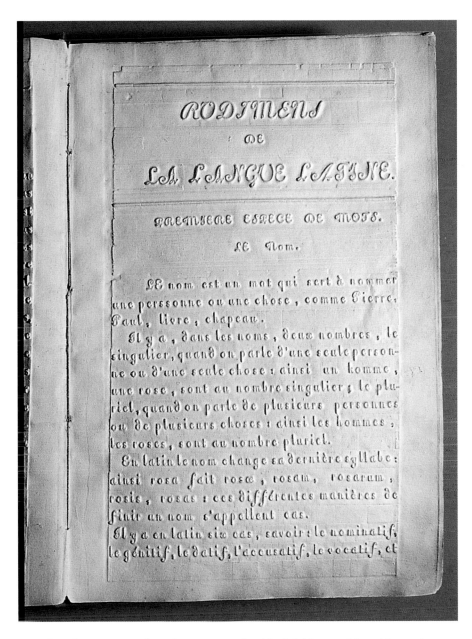

Print letters were embossed on paper so that blind children could read by touch. The type was composed and the pages were embossed by the blind children at the school with the advice of Clousier, the king's printer.

be to yield good characters in relief? How can the paper be kept from sticking to the metal type during embossing? (Dry soap was found to do the trick.) All these details had to be ironed out before embossed print could be produced. When these difficulties were overcome, it was relatively easy to train blind children to compose the lines and pages of type, and to use sturdy young men to operate the press [see illustration on page 51]. Since they could be embossed on one side only, pages were pasted back to back, and then bound together by sewing them between thick cardboard covers. *Voilà* — an embossed book.

For material to be read by both blind and sighted people, "Haüy Noire" was provided in which the embossed letters were also inked in black. This was done by placing a parchment sheet smeared with ink on top of the paper to be embossed.[41]

FINANCIAL WOES

One of the relentless challenges Haüy faced was how to keep the school afloat financially. An auspicious report issued early in 1785 by the Royal Academy of Sciences gave the school some much-needed early publicity. "We have seen this school," wrote the commissioners[42] appointed by the Academy, "which presents a curious and touching spectacle. Several

Valentin Haüy's "typesetting" technique.

young blind people of both sexes, taught by a master who is also blind, happily receive instruction that is given with particular care, and they all seem to applaud each other at having acquired this new way of life."[43]

The impact of the Academy's report was felt almost immediately: "The school for the blind became absolutely the rage. All classes of society were interested in the establishment, and each one strove to out-do the other. Eminent musicians and actors gave performances for its benefit. The Lyceum, the Museum, the Salon de Correspondence soon vied with one another for the privilege of having the young sightless pupils stammer (to borrow the expression of their instructor) the first elements of reading, arithmetic, history, geography, and music at their sessions; and these exercises were always concluded by collections for their benefit. Donations poured in from all sides, and the funds were placed in the treasury of the Philanthropic Society."[44]

Haüy did his part to sustain the fund-raising effort, organizing public demonstrations to showcase his best students. His most ambitious endeavor was a concert given before the royal family at Versailles on December 26th, 1786.[45] There, to the utter astonishment of the audience, twenty-four blind youngsters showed what they had learned. In a particularly dramatic moment, the king chose a book and dictated a phrase to a blind student, who wrote it down using Haüy's "typesetting" technique. The former beggar, François Le Sueur, who had been asked to leave the room, now re-entered and read aloud the phrase, which he could not possibly have heard. Later, Le Sueur performed some mathematical calculations, and other children read aloud from their embossed books. The audience was flabbergasted when a young sighted boy received a reading lesson from a blind student. Throughout this concert, members of the audience felt such tenderness for the children that tears flowed down many a cheek. The children were so beloved by the court that they were invited to stay a few more days as houseguests.[46]

These concerts were the high point of the school's early history. What better "word-of-mouth" could Haüy hope for? Henceforth, Haüy was permitted to call his school the Institution Royale des Jeunes Aveugles (Royal Institution for Blind Youth). But the situation was to deteriorate quickly as a bloody revolution convulsed France in 1789. The financial support the royal family promised did not materialize, and many wealthy philanthropists who had underwritten Haüy's work fled abroad — fearing for their fortunes, even their lives. Fervent revolutionaries belittled institutions for blind children and deaf-mutes as "infamous relics of absolutist charity and clerical superstition."[47] "Philanthropy, which has so lately been the fashion in Paris, gave place to a demoniac and blood-thirsty cruelty which has no parallel in the history of nations. The best blood of France flowed like water, and all thought of humanity seemed banished from the minds of the frantic barbarians who rule her."[48] The Philanthropic Society, which had taken charge of this noble enterprise from its inception, was broken up, its members exiled or imprisoned (many of those imprisoned were guillotined).[49]

Although the revolution sought to rebuild society on the principles of "Liberty, Equality, and Fraternity," in fact it proved disastrous for Haüy's own revolutionary idea of educating blind children to become full, self-supporting members of society.

NATIONALIZATION

Where would Haüy find sponsors now? The only feasible source of money was the government, and Haüy petitioned the Constituent Assembly for funding. It was granted, but at a price: the school was nationalized in July 1791. Furthermore, the school would have to merge with that for deaf-mutes, an arrangement that proved impossible. Inevitably, intense discord arose between Haüy and the ambitious, "stiff-necked"[50] priest, Abbé Roch Ambroise Sicard,[51] who headed up the school for deaf-mute children. The situation improved only temporarily in 1794, when the deaf-mutes moved to another location, and Haüy's school was moved to a hostel once used by a religious order, the Daughters of St. Catherine, as a night asylum for girls. There, a government policy of strict supervision of the students was imposed, as it was in all educational institutions at that time. Where previously both Haüy and Sicard had been relaxed in their oversight, now the children were watched constantly. At night, the dormitories were illuminated, and at each end of the chamber an adult supervisor had his or her bed.[52] This must have been particularly unnerving for the blind children, who could not see if they were being watched.

For lack of funds, Haüy was said to have eaten only one meal a day for a year in order that his students might not starve.[53] To add to his problems, those students who had completed their education but could not find jobs stayed on as "man-students," giving ammunition to his critics, who argued that blind children would always be wards of the state.

HYMNE
A L'ÊTRE SUPRÊME.

Paroles du Citoyen LAURENCE, *Député à la Convention Nationale.*

Musique du Citoyen GERSIN, *Second Instituteur des* AVEUGLES-TRAVAILLEURS.

PREMIER ŒUVRE DE MUSIQUE,

SORTI DE LA PRESSE

DE L'INSTITUT NATIONAL DES

AVEUGLES-TRAVAILLEURS,

DÉDIÉ

A LA CONVENTION NATIONALE,

For several years, profits from the printing shop helped raise needed funds for Haüy's school.[54] The blind students printed numerous bulletins, handbills, posters, and tracts, for which there was an insatiable demand during those anarchic, politically charged times.[55]

HAÜY JOINS THE REVOLUTION

Despite his early connections with royalty, Haüy had, by the 1790s, become an enthusiastic supporter of the revolution, assuming the position of secretary of the Arsenal Section Revolutionary Committee. He surely hoped that his actions would help his school survive amidst the dangers and uncertainties of the revolution, but in the long term his behavior proved damaging to himself and to the school. While at the Arsenal location, the school changed its name, once again, to the Institute for the Working Blind (Institut des Aveugles Travailleurs), a name bestowed upon the institute by members of the public who admired "the working blind" and wanted to differentiate them from indigent blind people.[56]

Haüy also became very involved with Théophilanthropy, a "natural religion"[57] that offered solace to people who felt a spiritual emptiness after the eclipse of the Roman Catholic church. (Some people considered Théophilanthropy a front for subversives, even a Masonic plot!)[58] Haüy held the first meeting of this new "church" in January 1797 at the Institute, which continued to serve as headquarters for the cult's management committee.[59] Haüy conducted the services dressed in a sky-blue tunic, pink sash, and white robe,[60] while the blind boys' choir sang. Napoleon Bonaparte would later sneer at this "religion in dressing gowns."[61]

RELOCATION TO THE QUINZE-VINGTS

Throughout the 18th century, and even beyond Napoleon's seizure of power, the public treasury was perilously short of money — in part a consequence of France's support of the American Revolution — and the question was raised as to why precious funds had to be used to support two organizations for the blind. Interior Minister Lucien Bonaparte, Napoleon's brother, thought it would make financial sense to combine Haüy's school with the Quinze-Vingts (see sidebar), a richly endowed asylum for indigent blind adults located in a former barracks with plenty of space.[62]

Getting wind of the proposal, Haüy realized that such a move would endanger his school and eliminate his autonomy. He criticized the proposal in three notes to officials, and, tactlessly, had his students print up a 16-page brochure opposing the government, which he distributed widely across Paris. Lucien Bonaparte was dismissed from his position (he was the only Bonaparte to disapprove of his brother's policies), and

Haüy's protests did not sit well with the new Interior Minister, Jean-Antoine Chaptal. In a stern repost to Haüy, he wrote: "Citizen: it is with as much pain as surprise that I saw in public circulation several documents in your name that are misleading about the government's policies…. Not only can such a provocation not be justified on any account, but it is reprehensible when it is put out by an instructor paid by the government and obliged by your status as well as your duty to conform to the administrative measure it believes should be adopted by the establishment you lead."[63]

Despite Haüy's determined efforts, the transfer was put into effect. On February 16, 1801, with no time to make preparations, the students were transferred, bag and baggage, to the Quinze-Vingts on rue de Charenton.

LIFE INSIDE THE QUINZE-VINGTS

Given the parlous state of the national treasury, the blind children were expected to pay their own way by producing saleable goods in workshops specially erected for them. Each day they labored for eight hours to spin carded wool, make sheets, and mill tobacco (even though it was against regulations). Only two hours a day were allotted for education.

The children were closely supervised at all times, to make sure they did not touch one another, which might lead to immoral behavior. (The easy-going Haüy had encouraged contact between the sexes and was proud of those students who married and formed their own families.)[64] "The fact of being forbidden to touch one another under any pretext imprisoned the students within themselves as effectively as if they had been sealed up inside the walls of the Quinze-Vingts."[65]

HAÜY IS OUSTED

Relieved of all administrative responsibilities once the move occurred, Haüy chafed under the new, top-down regulations issued by bureaucrats more concerned with process than with outcomes. Used to running his own show, and dismayed to see his dream of producing well-educated, self-supporting blind people shattered, Haüy engaged in passive resistance. Government regulations forbade the students to leave the enclosure of the Quinze-Vingts? Very well, Haüy had passes printed and signed by himself, authorizing the porter to let the students pass through the gates. The authorities wanted him to give religious instruction? Haüy used the allotted time to teach students about Rousseau and the religion of Théophilanthropy. Perhaps his most

egregious act was to sabotage the sale of woolen yarn made by the blind girls. He actually told manufacturers who had come to the Quinze-Vingts ready to buy that there was nothing to see, and that it was his property in any case.[66]

Haüy's rebellion made his position untenable. In April 1801, Chaptal wrote to the Quinze-Vingts agent-general, Charles Bouret,[67] "I know that citizen Haüy engages in all manner of intrigue. ...[A]t least firmly reproach citizen Haüy for his inconsiderate demeanor, and let him know that the eye of the Administration is watching him in a very particular manner."

Either Bouret did not warn Haüy or, more likely, Haüy paid no heed. On August 10, 1801, Bouret sent a desperate note to Chaptal: "Citizen, kindly tell me what repressive measures you think ought to be taken to bring to a halt the scandalous abuse that is the subject of this letter."[68]

Haüy was forced to retire in February 1802, at the age of 56, with an annual pension of 2,000 francs — somewhat less than one-half his salary.[69] Far from harming the children, Haüy's departure may have helped. Haüy was understandably concerned that governmental policies were not good for his students, but his impolitic behavior did not help him or

his students gain a sympathetic hearing from Interior Minister Chaptal.[70]

A NEW DIRECTOR

Within a year of Haüy's dismissal, Paul Seignette was appointed agent-general of the Quinze-Vingts. Only 33 years old, he was open-minded about how to educate blind children and smart enough to seek advice, including that of Haüy's first student, François Le Sueur. The punishing workshops were closed in 1811; they never turned a profit despite Chaptal's attempt to find a market for their products.

A new director of the Institution was appointed October 18, 1815. He was Sébastien Guillié, a medical doctor, who supervised the move to a new location in February 1816. The blind children would at last be released from their captivity in the Quinze Vingts.

Dating back to the 13th century, King Louis IX built a shelter for blind people, called the Quinze-Vingts. The principal work of the residents was begging for money, which was returned to the fraternity as a means of support. The Quinze-Vingts tried to avoid confrontations like this one by assigning begging spots. The elaborately decorated hurdy-gurdy sported by the beggar at the right suggests that he did very well from begging.

Touched by the hardships he witnessed among poor blind people in 13th-century Paris, King Louis IX ("Saint Louis") built a fraternal residence for 300 blind men and women called the Quinze-Vingts (the name follows the practice of counting in twenties: 15 x 20 = 300).[71] Few obligations were imposed upon the brothers and sisters, as they were called, although they had to swear to live, and die, in the Catholic faith, and pray regularly for the king, queen, royal family, and all benefactors.

Begging was encouraged as the primary means of supporting the residence. All alms had to be turned over to the treasury, but food received by a beggar was divided equally between the institution and the beggar. "For the Quinze-Vingts, God's bread!" was a familiar cry throughout Paris. Profitable spots were assigned in a highly organized manner, and the best ones could be rented. Quinze-Vingts beggars wore special insignia, giving them the status of "aristocrats of beggars."[72] Other residents ran taverns and small stores within the Quinze-Vingts precincts, or worked in the outside community as bell ringers or town criers — among the few jobs reserved for blind people. Over time, the management of the hospice became "quite democratic," and residents could save their own money, marry, and raise children.

After several generations, the Quinze-Vingts became wealthy from donations, bequests, legacies, rents, income from begging, and tax exemptions. By 1779 the charity "formed, in the center of Paris, a monument remarkable for the multiplicity and beauty of its buildings."[73] The site included a beautiful garden in which the blind residents could stroll in the warm weather, far from the confusion and ordure of the streets of Paris. Once a week, they were entertained by a military band.

Such opulence eventually aroused the envy of both the religious and secular powers, and with scarcely any warning,

near the end of 1779, Louis-René-Edouard de Rohan, Cardinal Bishop of Strasbourg, who as Grand Almoner was responsible for the Quinze-Vingts, successfully implemented his plan to sell the property and demolish the buildings.[74] The sale raised six million livres — one million of which was set aside to provide pensions for blind people and five million of which was rolled into the public treasury. In return for its cut, the government was obliged to make annual payments to the Quinze-Vingts of 250,000 livres, to this day regarded as a "public debt — none more sacred."[75]

Begging was now forbidden "on pain of imprisonment;" instead, a fixed pension was given to blind residents (as well as to some non-resident pensioners).[76] Residents were moved to a former barracks on rue de Charenton. It was here in 1801 that Valentin Haüy's students were forced to relocate and live in virtual imprisonment for another 15 years. None of the promised renovations were made; the holes and crevices in the walls of the boys' dormitory were big enough for "trouble makers" to hide in.[77] The dormitories were so cold, cramped, and humid that every morning dew-like moisture coated the blankets.[78] Discipline among the blind adults who were already living there was lax; drunken brawls were not uncommon. Residents kept rabbits, chickens, and pigeons in their small apartments, and dogs wandered about freely.

What began as a democratic, communal fraternity had, by the 19th century, been transformed into a secular, public institution supported by the government. In 1880, the Quinze-Vingts became a national medical center specializing in the prevention and treatment of eye conditions. It remains a residence for 200 blind people from all French territories.[79]

1. boys' staircase
2. girls' staircase
a. rue Saint-Victor entrance
b. great courtyard
c. walkways [for exercise]
d. linen room
e. baths
f. small weaving shop
g. print library
h. employees' refectory
i. large weaving shop
k. students' refectory
l. chapel
m. basket-making
n. mat-making (straw)
o. mat-making (wool)
p. mat-making (rush)
q. packing/boxes
r. knitting
s. reading room for the sighted
t. harmony classroom
u. math classroom
v. director's classroom
   (history and modern languages)
x. second instructor's classroom
   (ancient languages and geography)
y. repetition of reading in relief
aa. large corridor (adjacent building)
bb. library of books in relief
cc. printing presses
dd. piano classroom
ee. organ classroom
ff. second math classroom
gg. second piano classroom

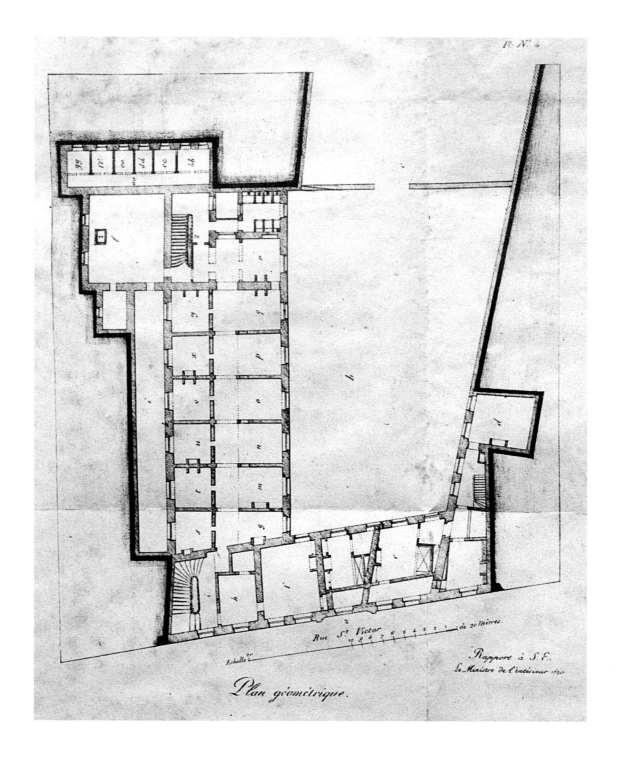

SCHOOL LIFE

The director who welcomed Louis Braille in February 1819 was Sébastien Guillié, a 38-year-old former military doctor and a discreet royalist with impeccable manners. Appointed Instituteur in chief on April 21, 1814, Guillié's first challenge would be the transfer of the blind children from the Quinze-Vingts as soon as a suitable building could be found. (By suitable, Guillié meant a building in which the sexes could be segregated.)

The move was delayed when Napoleon temporarily regained power for 100 days in the spring of 1815, and the nation was again mobilized for war. After Napoleon's defeat at Waterloo, the Bourbon monarchy was restored to the throne and Guillié could move ahead with his plans. The school relocated to 68 rue Saint-Victor[2] on February 20, 1816. There, Guillié set out to reverse the setbacks suffered by the blind children during their incarceration at the Quinze-Vingts, where their education was neglected and they were often exposed to the uncouth blind adults living there. "Everything had to be re-done after the move...," he complained, "but the most urgent priority was to restore morale to the Institution."[3]

Facing page:
Inside this labyrinthine building, Louis Braille received a good education, developed his musical talents, became a much-loved teacher, and devised a reading and writing system for the world's blind people.

A HOST OF OBSTACLES

Funds for the new Institution Royale des Jeunes Aveugles were provided by the Interior Ministry, with a budget of 50,000 francs.[4] From this modest sum, Guillié had to pay salaries, feed students and some employees, remodel the building, install workshops, buy equipment and musical instruments, obtain a new set of type for embossed printing, improve ventilation to reduce odors from the cesspit, and overcome what he called "a host of obstacles."[5] Constrained by limited funds, Guillié made every effort to keep costs down. To conserve cooking fuel, he experimented with a pressure cooker that prepared nutritious food more quickly.[6] He grumbled that the budget would not allow him to buy more wine, which was added to the water the students drank in the belief that it would give them strength.[7] He initiated the construction of the Institution's own chapel, which he considered essential to the spiritual well-being of his charges, and hired a chaplain.

Although Guillié boasted of many successes, his reports to the Interior Minister should be taken with a grain of salt because, while intelligent and capable, Guillié was "something of a charlatan."[8] His basic approach to running the Institution was to do whatever made him look good.[9]

HARSH DISCIPLINE

Before moving to the new location, Guillié had to weed out any students who, because of bad behavior or poor health, could not be allowed into the new building.[10] Upon those who were accepted, Guillié imposed the strictest discipline, shocking to modern sensibilities but common at that time. In his 1818 report to the Interior Minister, Guillié made this dubious assertion to justify his harsh policies: "It has been clearly shown that the blind are not like other people, [who are] susceptible to being restrained by external demonstrations. [The blind] appreciate things only by extremes, and can understand justice only by its effects. A paternal and just management has thus replaced the flexible and weak regime that has for so long prevented good from being done."[11]

A frequent punishment in French schools at that time was to lock unruly children in a dark closet, but this held little terror for children who couldn't see. Misbehaved children were put on dry bread and water, physically punished, and confined to the building.[12] Boys were whipped and, in extreme cases, chained to an iron ring fixed to a post. The girls were treated no better. One girl was sick for five months after being whipped.[13] It is unlikely that Louis Braille escaped punishment — his happy-go-lucky (*gai*)

ALLANT A L'ÉCOLE

"Going to School"

and teasing (*taquin*) temperament did not always please his teachers.[14]

MUTUAL INSTRUCTION

The school now housed some 90 students (60 boys and 30 girls), who were required to attend both academic classes and workshops.[15] A typical day was 15 hours long, divided among intellectual work, music, manual work, meals, recreation, and religious devotions. Students were supervised closely and forbidden to move anywhere in the building without displaying their assigned numbers on a medallion worn on a ribbon around their necks. Louis was number 70.

Instruction was primarily oral, with a heavy emphasis on rote learning and memorization. To Haüy's collection of raised-letter books, Guillié added more than 1,720 volumes to the library, using a modified typeface scarcely more readable than Haüy's original font. Most of the books were religious in nature and few were practical — Greek and Latin, algebra, Spanish, Italian, and English grammar — for blind people seeking skills that might lead to employment.[16] Years later, when Guillié's deputy, Pierre-Armand Dufau, had become director, he sarcastically remarked that the school turned out beggars who knew Latin and geometry.[17]

There were three teachers, all sighted, for ninety students: two men, Guillié and Dufau, and one woman, Zélie Cardeilhac. These three instructors taught six other "teachers" drawn from among the most capable blind students, who in turn taught the most advanced of the others. These became assistants (*répétiteurs*) — in effect apprentice teachers. There was one additional level: some of the youngest students were selected to teach for only eight days, after which they were replaced. Virtually everyone was both teacher and student.[18]

MUSIC FLOURISHES
Guillié was a fine musician and reintroduced the teaching of music to all students.[19] Despite his limited budget, the director purchased many musical instruments — violins, cellos, one double bass, clarinets, oboes, bassoons, flutes, guitars, and a second organ for students

LE CHIEN DE L'AVEUGLE.

A blind person who was an able musician — usually on a fiddle or hurdy-gurdy — could get by. A pleasing appearance, good musicianship, jocular personality, and a cute dog made it easier to charm money from bystanders.

to practice on. The director donated three pianos, bringing the total to eight.[20] In the chapel, there was also a two-manual, two wind chest organ with 16 stops and an octave of pedals, which students played during services.[21] Guillié hoped that children from the larger towns might find jobs as organists when they returned home. Children from smaller towns were taught to play a versatile woodwind instrument called a serpent, which was a useful accompaniment to plainsong.

Professional musicians from around Paris flocked to the school, volunteering to give blind children a musical education. Niccoló Paganini, the Italian virtuoso violinist and composer, declared that he had never had an adequate notion of harmony until he heard the blind students perform.[22] Louis Braille benefited enormously from the music programs, not only because he loved music, but also because he could supplement his income as an organist, playing in one of the more prestigious churches, Saint-Nicolas-des-Champs, from 1834 to 1839.

LEARNING A TRADE

Practical classes in knitting, making slippers, chair caning, basket making, and the like, were offered so that students might earn a living and become independent once they completed their eight-year stint at the Institute. Such instruction

CHAISIER

Chair caning was performed by touch alone. Those made at the Institution were "coarse chairs" used in churches and public walks.

was a feature of schools for the blind around the world. Those who lived near the sea were taught to make fishing nets, and those from port towns learned how to make ropes. Several students knitted waistcoats, shirts, and petticoats for hosiers in Paris, "which give the greatest satisfaction," Guillié claimed.[23] One product all students were required to make was straw and rush mats because "they are sure articles of sale in almost every part of France."[24] Plush shoes sold well, especially in winter.

As far back as 1786, blind youngsters had learned the art of printing — for both raised-letter and inkprint books. Indeed, the trade of printer was one in which a blind boy could do well. However, for reasons related to Napoleon's strict censorship of the press[25] and determination to control all printing, the director-general of printing and bookselling ordered the Institution's printing shop destroyed — a policy implemented "without pity" in 1812.[26] "In consequence of this act of cruelty," Guillié recorded, "these unfortunate beings lost the means of learning a business, which put them in the way of gaining a livelihood better than any other,"[27] and the Institution lost a source of considerable revenue.[28] Indeed, except for printing, the workshops never reaped the rewards Guillié had hoped. His reports show that annual sales of

items made by the students amounted to only a few hundred francs (roughly 1% of revenues).

GUILLIÉ SHOWS OFF HIS STUDENTS

In 1817, Guillié wrote and published a book on educating the blind that was so popular it was re-issued in 1819 and again in 1820, and was translated into English and German.[30] As always, Guillié liked to make a good impression, and the beautiful engravings of his students are idealized. To be fair, the purpose of these kinds of publications was to elicit public support. The engravings depict the students as smartly dressed, well groomed, and healthy. In truth, many children were in poor health, and some bore the scars of smallpox. While blindness was depicted in these drawings by the convention of closed eyes, it is more likely the students' eyes would have been open and damaged or deformed, as was the case with Louis Braille. (It was customary during public demonstrations to cover the students' eyes with ribbons, to spare the sensibilities of ladies in the audience.)

A GRUESOME EXPERIMENT

Patients in public hospitals were frequently used for medical experiments, and even 19th-century blind children suffered at the hands of their supposed protectors. Sebastian Guillié performed a cruel experiment on his blind charges to advance his reputation as a doctor. He obtained permission from the Hospital for Sick Children to extract pus from the eyes of children suffering from a purulent eye disease, blepharo-blenorrhea, and placed it in the eyes of four indigent blind children under his care at the Institution. He hoped to prove that this condition was contagious rather than epidemic. His pitiless logic was that it would be inhumane to do this to sighted children, who could become blind, but little harm would come to those already without sight.

It took 40 days for the disease to run its course, during which time the children suffered burning sensations in their eyes, violent pain in the eyelids, and such pressure that the eye felt as if it would explode. In the mornings, the children's eyelids were sealed so tightly that the eyelashes were painfully pulled out in forcing the eyes open.[29]

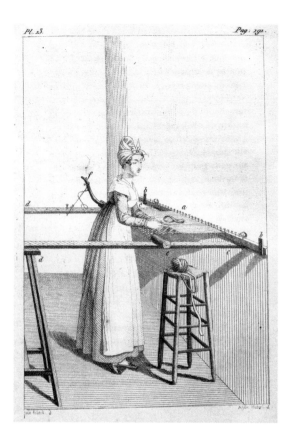

Using strips of colored cloth, this woman weaves a floor covering. Both sexes were taught this trade. As the carpet is woven, it is wound around the wooden cylinder visible beneath her right hand. This skill was introduced to the school "of late," i.e., about 1816. The students made a "vast number" of all sizes that were bought by many benevolent people, hoping that others would follow their example.

All the students were taught to make carpets out of straw or rushes because they were inexpensive and could be sold wherever in France the student lived.

Fur-lined slippers sold well, especially in winter. Louis Braille became foreman of the slipper workshop at age 14. Slippers were made inside-out on a stringed frame, so the fur lining could be easily attached.

Engravings from Sébastien Guillié's *Essay on the Instruction and Amusements of the Blind* (1817).

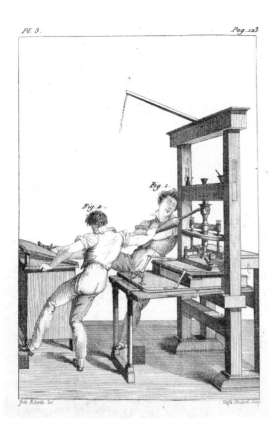

Printing was a trade at which blind boys could be very successful. It took the strength of two young men to produce enough pressure to emboss print into dampened paper.

With minor adaptations, weaving could be done by blind people. Different colors of thread were indicated by notches cut in the end of the shuttle. As the Industrial Revolution gained speed, textile production was mechanized and moved from the domestic hearth into newfangled steam-powered factories, limiting job opportunities for blind people.

Blind teachers were better than those with sight at teaching blind children to knit. Children who at home could not produce a single stitch, could knit garters after only a few days of instruction.

Despite years of training and impressive public demonstrations of blind people nimbly performing various trades, the reality of employment for blind graduates was sobering. Writing anonymously for *North American Review* in 1833, Samuel Gridley Howe, head of the newly founded New-England Institution for the Education of the Blind in Boston (now Perkins School for the Blind) and a practical Yankee, speculated, "How many of those who leave the institution at the expiration of their time are enabled to gain their own livelihood?"

"Not one in twenty" was his startling conclusion.[31] In his *Address to the Trustees* written that same year, Howe gave his candid impressions of the Paris school at the time Louis Braille was there:

"The Institution for the Education for the Blind in Paris, as it is the oldest, and as there is about it more of show and parade than any other in Europe, has also the reputation of being the best; but if one judges the tree by its fruit, and not by its flowers and foliage, this will not be his conclusion.

"Its founder and the great benefactor of the blind, Abbé Haüy [Howe confuses Valentin with his brother, René-Just], invented and put into practice many contrivances for the education of the blind; and otherwise rendered the institution excellent for the age, and the time it had existed; but as he left it so it has remained. The great fault in the Parisian institution is the diversity of employment to which the pupils are put; and the effort made to enable them to perform surprising but useless tricks. The same degree of intellectual education is given to all, without reference to their destination in life; and a poor boy, who is to get his livelihood by weaving or whip makeup, is as well instructed in mathematics, and polite literature, as he who is to pursue a literary career. Now there is no reason why a shoe maker or a basket maker should not be well-educated; provided he can learn his profession thoroughly, and find the necessary leisure to study."[32]

READING AND WRITING BEFORE THE BRAILLE CODE

Reading and writing for blind children in the early-19th century remained completely unsatisfactory, despite Haüy's innovations. True, Guillié had built up the school's library of embossed books, but at 4.5 kilos (about 9 pounds) each,

The dashing Samuel Gridley Howe, the first director of what is now the Perkins School for the Blind in Boston, Mass., visited the Paris Institute in the 1830s, when Louis was a student there.

they were too heavy to hold, rest on a lap, or carry about. Countless ingenious attempts, in France and elsewhere, to improve upon Haüy's embossed print were tried and quickly rejected as impractical.[33] One fundamental defect could never be remedied: embossed print is simply too hard to read by touch. Only a few students successfully mastered the art, one of whom was Louis Braille.

Writing techniques of the time were equally ill-suited to the physiology of touch. To learn to write, a blind child at the school would hold a stylus — a metal rod with a rounded tip — and trace the shapes of letters engraved into a metal sheet. Once the student had learned to recognize and remember the sensations produced in the muscles, he or she was ready to try to replicate the letter shapes on a separate piece of paper with a pencil. Writing with ink was not feasible at all; the finger that detected the motion of the tip of the pen ended up smearing the ink. Furthermore, the writer could not be certain the ink was flowing.

To write longhand, a blind person needed a way to move precisely from one line to the next, to avoid writing over previously written work. One way to accomplish this was with a handguide, a simple wooden frame with parallel, horizontal lines of wire or catgut stretched across it. Writing in this

Above: Engraved letters and symbols were used in the late-18th and early-19th centuries to familiarize young blind people with the shapes of print letters of the alphabet. Note that there is no "w" in the lower case letters. This letter is used infrequently in French, and Louis Braille was not familiar with it.

Below: A blind boy learns to feel, and then remember, the movements of a stylus as it traces the shapes of letters engraved in a metal plate. It is possible that the teacher depicted here is Guillié himself.

Left: This particular handguide had wires or catgut stretched across the page to prevent the writer's pencil from straying into lines previously used or not yet used.

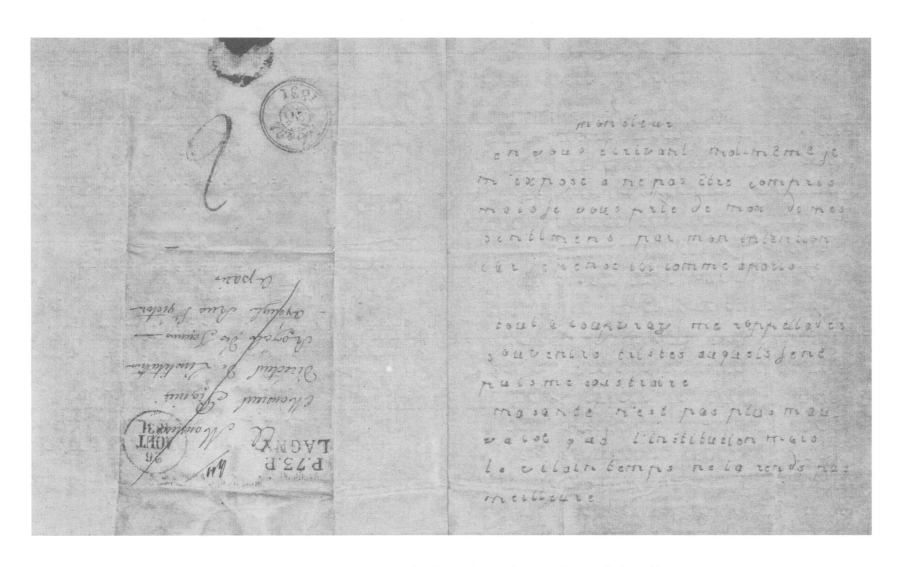

This is the handwriting of Louis Braille, blind since the age of three. It shows well-formed letters, even down to such details as accents and apostrophes, but little punctuation and no capital letters. Since he could not read what he had written, intense concentration was required, yet he rarely made mistakes. Only a small minority of blind children ever learned to produce legible handwriting.

manner required intense concentration. Abbé Charles Carton, director of the Bruges Institution for the Blind and Deaf-Mutes, and an acquaintance of Louis Braille, once asserted that only three or four blind people in Paris knew how to write.[34] We know Louis Braille was one because several letters written in his own hand have survived. His handwriting is well formed and legible.

Another writing technique was akin to assembling words with Scrabble tiles. Guillié used this method to impress the general public during frequent exhibitions that were held at the school. Indeed, under his leadership, the primary focus of instruction was to produce students who could perform well at public events; one of his earliest actions was to increase the capacity of the auditorium where the exercises were held from 280 to 400 seats.[35]

LOUIS EXCELS

Into this harsh environment stepped ten-year-old Louis Braille. At first, like all new students, Louis had to be guided around the large building by another blind student or one of a half-dozen sighted boys. (Sighted children were accepted into the school, where they received a free education in exchange for such services as sighted guide, scribe, or assistant to blind pupils in the printing

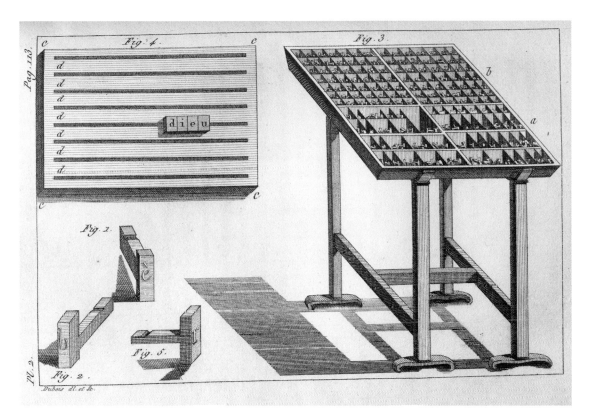

One method of writing was similar to Scrabble. Raised wooden letters were inserted by the blind writer into slots in a wooden case and read by touch.

shop.) Louis proved adept at forming a mental map of the five-floor building and was soon finding his own way around. Although Braille had probably never met another blind person before coming to the school, he made lifelong friends there, among them Gabriel Gauthier, a fellow student and outstanding musician and composer who eventually became director of the school's orchestra.

Louis proved competent at anything he tried. Braille's mentor, Dr. Alexandre François-René Pignier, director of the school from 1821 to 1840, wrote of Braille, "Endowed with great facility, with a lively intelligence, and above all with a remarkable soundness of mind, Braille became well known for his progress and success in his studies. His literary or scientific compositions included nothing but precise thoughts; they were distinguished by a great clarity of ideas expressed in a clear and correct style. You could recognize imagination there, but it was always directed by good sense."[36]

Pignier lists the prizes Louis won between 1820 and 1825: grammar, history, geography, geometry and algebra. His musical talent was recognized with prizes for cello and piano.[37] A visitor attending an awards ceremony in 1825 observed:

"...one student, Louis Braye[38] [sic] from the Department of Seine-et-Marne himself received five first prizes: amplification,[39] general grammar, geography, history, and mathematics. The books that comprised the prizes he had won, piled up with assiduous care behind him on the bench he occupied, soon formed a pyramid whose apex was much higher than the laureate's head."[40]

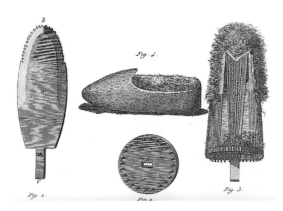

The style of slipper made at the Institution.

By 1826, while still a student, he was teaching algebra, grammar, and geography to other students, both blind and sighted. He attended courses at the Collège de France, studied the organ, and gave piano lessons to the younger pupils.[41] Endowed with leadership skills and nimble fingers, Louis was made foreman of the slipper workshop at age 14. The manual skills he had honed as a child, making colored fringes for harnesses, probably contributed to his early promotion.

NIGHT WRITING

Louis Braille's life, and that of all blind people, was to change forever when a former artillery captain, Nicolas-Marie-Charles Barbier de la Serre, showed up at the school in 1820 to present a new method of reading and writing for the blind.

Born May 18, 1767, into a family of minor aristocrats, Barbier trained at the royal military school at Brienne and began his career as an artillery officer. His life took an unconventional turn during the French Revolution, when he fled to America and worked as a surveyor. Insatiably curious, Barbier was intrigued by the exotic writing systems used by Native American tribes, among which he had spent some time. "Of all the inventions honoring the human spirit," wrote

Barbier, "writing has contributed most to its development and progress."[42] On his return to France early in the 19th century, he dedicated his time and talent to developing, among other things, methods for writing in code.

Barbier originally developed his "night writing" system as a way to transmit orders during night maneuvers. When the military authorities showed no interest, he began looking for other applications. By 1815, he was convinced his system would be helpful to "those born blind... who are deprived of the means of ever being able to read our books or our writing, and besides this, meeting with the greatest difficulties in correctly tracing the outlines of [print] letters."[43] By the time Barbier arrived at the Institution Royale des Jeunes Aveugles in late 1820, he had experimented with several versions of his night-writing code and had designed a simple writing device — the prototype of the slate and stylus still widely used by blind people.

Guillié was not overly impressed with this new dot system, but agreed to let the students try it out. The experiment evidently did not go well because Guillié refused to adopt Barbier's method.[44] Barbier later complained that Guillié's lack of interest stemmed from the code's simplicity, "which concealed its advantages [from him]." In fact, in Barbier's opinion, the Institution's public demonstrations of the students' skills had become nothing more than occasions to further Guillié's personal vanity.[45]

Accustomed to giving orders as an artillery officer, Barbier was not easily deterred and returned to the Institution to press his case. To his surprise, he was informed that Guillié had been fired over a "scandalous" relationship with the much younger chief instructress, Zélie Cardeilhac, a music teacher who had come over from the Quinze-Vingts in 1816. An accomplished musician, she taught harmony, piano to the girls, and concert harp to the boys — an instrument Guillié claimed was difficult even for those with sight.[46]

Taking Guillie's place as director after this unexpected turn of events was Alexandre François-René Pignier, a gentle, devout, somewhat formal man, who was to play a vital role in Louis Braille's development of a new system of literacy for blind people around the world.

Captain Charles Barbier, a former artillery officer, devised a system of writing and reading with embossed dots that he hoped the army could use to send messages undetected at night because no light was needed to read or write them.

Charles Barbier de la Serre.
Capitaine d'Artillerie.

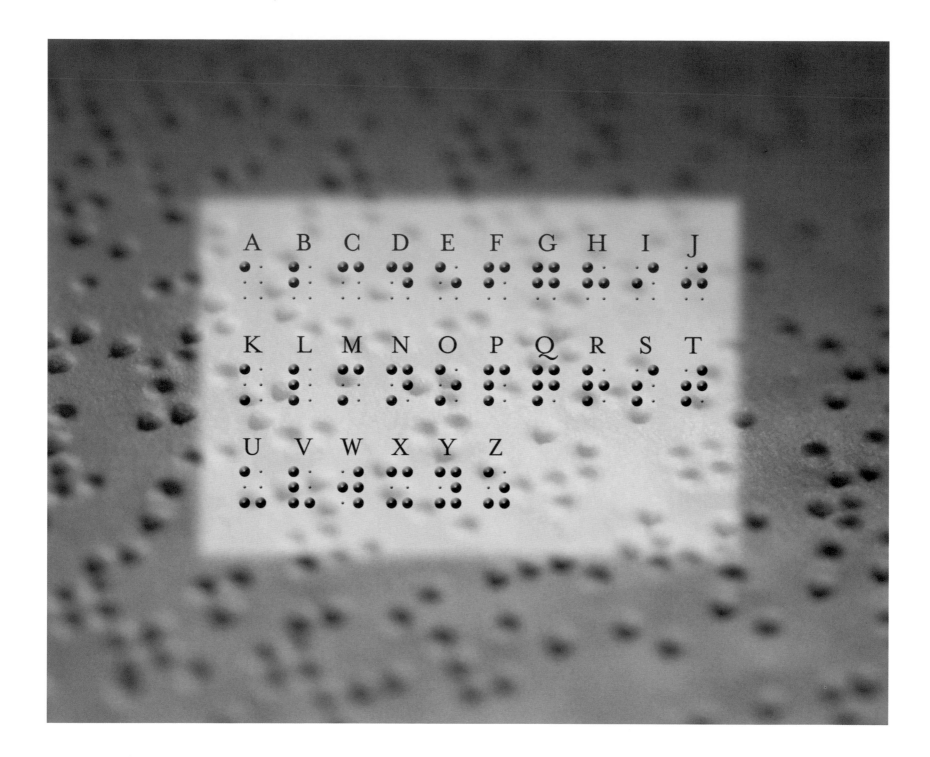

BRAILLE CODE

Dr. Pignier was shocked by what he discovered during his first day as director, February 20, 1821. As a medical doctor,[2] he realized that the dank and poorly ventilated building was undermining the health of the students. The children whom Dr. Guillié had described as "chubby for the most part" in his reports to the Interior Ministry[3] were, in fact, noticeably weak from malnutrition. The sound of coughing reverberated through the corridors. To obtain an objective assessment of the situation, Pignier commissioned a report on the children's health from two independent doctors.

Facing page:
By age 16, Louis Braille had figured out this code that could be read by touch. His configurations of raised dots opened the door to literacy and culture for blind people around the world.

> "The first thing that struck us was the deathly white complexion and sickly appearance of most of [the students]. Several show signs of scrofula [tuberculosis]; some even have swollen glands. Many, especially the girls, have poor digestions, a condition rare among adolescents, and whose cause we can find in the [building and surrounding area]."[4]

A FRESH APPROACH

Dr. Pignier spent the next two decades, from 1821 to 1840, begging government officials to provide healthier quarters for the students. His relentless pleas were ignored, but he did what he could to improve the children's environment through better diet and outdoor exercise. Samuel Gridley Howe, who was conducting research in Europe before taking up the post of director of a newly founded school for the blind in Boston, visited the Paris institution, and was impressed by the students' outdoor excursions:

"I have often observed with a delighted eye the movement of the blind boys in Paris as they leave the Institution to go to play; each grasps a cord held by a seeing boy, and follows him rapidly and unhesitatingly through narrow streets, until they enter the immense 'Garden of Plants,'[5] when quitting the string they run away among the trees, and frolic and play together with all the zest and enjoyment of seeing children. They know every tree and shrub, they careen it up one alley and down another, they chase, catch, overthrow and knock each other about, exactly like seeing boys; and to judge by their laughing faces, their wild and unrestrained gestures, and their loud and hearty shouts, they partake equally [in] the delightful exitement [sic] of boyish play."[6]

BARBIER'S INVENTION

Pignier had been director for only a short time when Captain Barbier contacted him about the raised-dot reading and writing system he had shown to Guillié. Pignier knew the reading and writing techniques currently in use were ineffective and that the only people qualified to judge the merits of any proposed system were the blind children themselves. He reported to the administration, "I am eager to try this method; time will teach us what advantages can be obtained from it."[11]

Just before the summer break in 1821, Pignier assembled the students to describe Barbier's *écriture nocturne* (night writing) system, and to let them experiment with samples of embossed pages that Barbier had left at the Institution.[12] The students immediately recognized that the raised dots were easier to read than the tactually ambiguous lines and curves that made up print letters in relief.

REPUBLIQUE FRANÇAISE
25F +10F
POSTES
1745   1822
VALENTIN HAÜY

HAÜY IS REMEMBERED

After Valentin Haüy was forced to retire in February 1802, he had been invited by Czar Alexander I of Russia to set up a school for blind children in St. Petersburg. He had little success.[7] At the age of 72, he returned to Paris, destitute and in poor health, and moved in with his brother, Abbé René-Just, who had a small attic apartment just a few blocks from the school. Refuting the notion that the "revolutionary" Haüy posed a threat, the kindly Dr. Pignier organized a concert in Haüy's honor at the school on August 21, 1821.[8] The classrooms and dining rooms were brightly decorated for the occasion, and a grateful Haüy spent the entire day dining and chatting happily with "his children." Overcome by emotion, Haüy could manage only a brief response: "My dear children, it is God who has done everything."[9] (Louis Braille, only 12 years old, must have participated in the celebration, but there is no evidence that he actually met Haüy.)[10] Less than a year later, in March 1822, Haüy died.

BARBIER'S CODE

Barbier's system relied on a 12-dot cell: two vertical columns of six dots each. His code was not based on the alphabet, rather it was based on sounds — a process that was difficult for the reader, and not at all analogous to the way print is read.

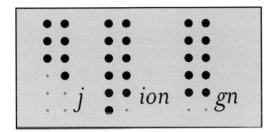

The students were, at first, enthusiastic about this new system, which was a distinct improvement over raised letters. Armed with the lightweight slates, a stylus, and a few sheets of paper, they could take notes, put their own thoughts on paper, and jot down reminders to themselves.[13] Barbier was further emboldened when his new dot system earned a bronze medal in 1823 at the prestigious Exposition of Products of French Industry. Official recognition soon followed from the Royal Academy of Sciences, which issued a favorable and prescient report in December 1823 that stated, "[O]rdinary writing is the art of speaking to the eyes. What Mr. Barbier has found is the art of speaking to the touch."[14]

But the fatal flaws in Barbier's system could not be ignored: There was no spelling, no grammar, no way to represent numbers, no music. Although the students could read and write, in a manner of speaking, they could never become literate in the way sighted people are.

Only one small book was ever embossed using Barbier's code, *Recueil d'anecdotes, extrait de la morale en action* (Collection of Anecdotes Teaching Moral Lessons, 1827). A transcription (below) of a few pages from the book demonstrates how much space it took up — only nine short lines at most per page.

Transcription from Recueil d'anecdotes[15]

English: A woman had been widowed with three sons and was provided for only by their work.

French: Une femme était restée veuve avec trois garçons et ne subsistait que par leur travail.

Transcription of Barbier's Code
....un
fam ètè résté veuve a-
vec troi garson é
n subsistè q d
leur travall

Barbier broke the French language down into 36 syllables, vowels, and consonants, all of which fit into a 6x6 grid. It was numbered 1-6 vertically to indicate row, and 1-6 horizontally for columns.

To use Barbier's system, the reader would first count the number of raised dots in each column: The number of dots in the left column indicated the row in Barbier's grid; the number of dots in the right column indicated the column in the grid. The two coordinates located one sound or character. So, for example, if the first column in a cell contained 6 dots and the next column contained 5, the configuration stood for the fifth symbol in the sixth row of the grid, that is, the syllable *ion*. To read with any speed at all, the blind reader had to memorize the entire grid, but memorization was a particular skill of blind students.

BARBIER'S SLATE

This lightweight, portable slate was far superior to the crude device Barbier first designed. The thin metal sheet, with rectangular apertures the size of the 12-dot cell, was attached by hinges to a wooden board with six grooves running along its length. The openings allowed a writer, using a stylus with a rounded tip, to position dots very precisely on the paper inserted between the metal sheet and the grooved board. Writing had to be pressed into the paper from right to left; when the paper was turned over, the raised dots would be read from left to right.

A charitable man, Barbier had some of the first tools fabricated by a carpenter who had succeeded in practicing his trade even after he became totally blind.[16] This handy writing tool and other aids were probably thought up by the blind readers themselves.[17]

ÉBÉNISTE

BRAILLE INVENTS BRAILLE

It was the inclusion of the astute Louis Braille among the young testers that changed the course of history. All the students eventually became aware of the limitations of Barbier's method, but it was Louis who figured out how to redesign it to create a user-friendly means of reading and writing. According to Pignier, Louis "with characteristic sagacity... indicated several improvements to M. Barbier, and

Carpenters could produce beautiful objects without eyesight. Such skilled artisans fabricated the wooden slates that blind people used, and which required great precision to properly position the raised dots.

resolved several difficulties with this writing that M. Barbier had been trying to solve for a long time."[18] Although there is no record of their actual conversation, it is unlikely that the irascible middle-aged captain took kindly to the blind teenager's criticism of his work.

Over the course of the next three years, from 1821 to 1824, Louis plugged away at defining and refining his own system. He took from Barbier the ideas of raised dots and use of a code; everything else was Louis's own invention. Pignier, who became Louis's mentor and friend, captured his devotion to the task at hand: "Braille, who was detained by classes for part of the day, experimented with his method in the early morning, when there were no distractions, and sometimes during the night when he couldn't sleep. He took paper, stylus and slate, his work tools, to the dormitory and slept among them."[19] Louis spent his summers and school vacations in Coupvray, where "the good country people would smile, perhaps with bemusement, when they saw him [sitting on a slope close to his house,] 'pecking at the paper....'"[20]

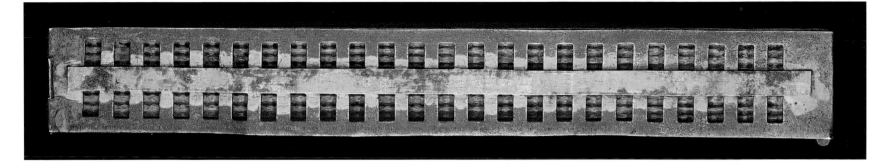

By age 15, Louis had cut Barbier's twelve-dot cell in half, to six dots, which fit neatly under a reader's fingertip. Originally, he had included dashes but abandoned that idea because dashes were difficult to write, and could be mistaken by the finger for two dots side by side. All the reader had to do to identify a character was to detect the presence or absence of dots within the six-dot cell.

The braille cell — an arrangement of 6 dots, 2 across and 3 down — is the basic unit of the braille code. Sixty-three patterns are mathematically possible[21] with six dots, sufficient to represent all letters, numbers, accents, and punctuation marks (see sidebar, next page). Braille would use this same cell for music and math. Further refinements, especially space-saving abbreviations (contractions) would come later, but Braille had laid the foundation of literacy for generations of blind people. The simplicity and versatility of his primary code is wholly original.

Because Louis's code proved much easier to write than that of Barbier, slates for writing it were ingeniously, and economically, made by soldering a strip of metal on the front of existing Barbier slates. The slate now produced two lines of six-dot cells instead of one line of twelve-dot cells. Space was added at the top and bottom of each cell to make up for the space blocked by the strip.

As Henri put it, "Braille did more than perfect Barbier's system, he modified it to the very foundation... Barbier still had his eyes; Braille had no more than his finger. From that came the six-dot cell that is so perfectly adapted to the requirements of the sense of touch: one dot higher, one dot wider, and the sign became scarcely readable."[22]

PIGNIER AS AMANUENSIS

The design of Braille's code was virtually completed by 1825, when he was only 16 years old. To reach this stage, Louis had carried out numerous experiments, given much thought to his procedure, and engaged in lengthy discussions with his blind friends, making good use of the perfectionism he had developed at his father's side. Pignier himself wrote down

the code that Louis had developed, "At last, Braille composed a description of his procedure for writing by means of dots, which the author of this report remembers writing down as [Braille] dictated it."[23] Braille himself taught the system to the students, and they quickly grasped its merits:

"[I]t allowed the teachers to take notes, the students to work in class in the same manner as those who had eyesight, and their compositions were judged on the copy they had written. They took down extracts from the best authors, and some compiled libraries of a great number of volumes for their own use. At last, they could in no time teach themselves the most difficult parts of a piece of music and the most complicated [works] of the great masters, which had hitherto

The logic Braille used to construct the code was ingenious in its simplicity. The user has to learn only ten different arrangements of dots within the cell:

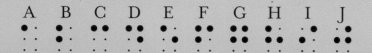

The adjacent dot configurations represent the first ten letters of the alphabet: *a–j*. The next ten letters of the alphabet, *k–t*, are the same as the first ten, except that dot 3 is added to each one.

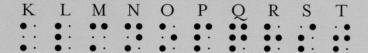

Finally, the letters *u, v, x, y* and *z* are formed by adding dots 3 and 6 to each cell, like this:

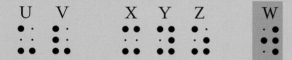

Only the letter *w* does not fit this scheme. Words with *w* were originally words imported into French, mainly for proper names, e.g., Watteville, Westphalia, Washington. Since Louis's handwritten letters never used capital letters, perhaps he was unaware of the *w*. Henry Hayter, an English friend and fellow organist who had studied in Paris, later pointed out this omission to Braille, who added *w* to the end of line 3 (the code for letter *x* had already been assigned the position that *w* would logically have occupied).

To capitalize a letter, one simply placed a dot 6 in front of it, like this:

CAPITAL SIGN

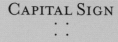

Later, in 1832, Louis created a number sign — dots 3,4,5,6 — which, when placed in front of the first ten letters of the alphabet, converts those letters to numbers. Thus, the number sign placed before *a* becomes *1*, before *b* becomes *2*, and so on.

Punctuation was formed by using dots in the lower part of the cell: dots 2,3,5, and 6, like this:

COMMA   QUESTION MARK   HYPHEN

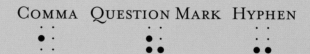

Braille's original code used the lower part of the cell for common mathematical symbols — plus, minus, multiplication, equals. Since then, the braille math code has been substantially revised.

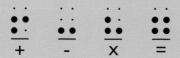

taken up much time. They could write down their literary and musical inspirations as they composed them, and so did not forget them."[24]

Four years later, in 1829, Braille's primary code was published by the school in embossed print with braille examples.[25] In the preface, Braille generously credited Charles Barbier: "If we have shown the advantages of our system over that of this inventor, we should like to say in his honor that it is his system that first gave us the idea of our own."[26] Although Braille's code has undergone modification and refinement over the years, particularly with the addition of space-saving contractions, his first published version is identical to the braille system used around the world today.

A LETTER TO BARBIER

An undated letter Braille wrote to Barbier has survived. It was never mailed, and Braille may have dropped it off at Barbier's house on rue Chanoinesse, not more than a twenty-minute walk[27] from the school. Before closing, Braille politely expressed his hope that the two could meet to discuss a new way of using raised dots, probably the decapoint method he used to write this very letter.

Sir, I came several times to your house without having the honor of finding you there. However I would like to submit to you a new application of [raised] dots in order to obtain your advice based on your long experience; I can easily write your procedure using three dots [28] *with the apparatus I have used to write this letter.*

I am going to take a little trip and I will have the honor of passing by your home at the beginning of November.

Accept, Sir, the expression of the profound respect with which I have the honor to be your very humble servant.

Although Barbier continued to work on his own code, he eventually came to appreciate Louis's achievement. On March 1, 1833, he wrote to Louis, now 24, "I cannot praise too highly the kind feelings which prompt you to be useful to those who share your misfortune... much can be expected of the enlightened sentiments which guide you."

That same year, on May 15, in a letter to Louis Braille, Barbier told the young teacher that he planned to include the following acknowledgment in a revised version of the manual for his own system: "It is M. Louis Braille, a young student at the Royal Institution in Paris, who first had the happy idea of using a ruler with three lines on it for writing raised dots. The characters take up less space and are easier to read. For these two reasons, he rendered a great service for which we are indebted to him."[29]

In a letter written when he was 22, Louis mocked his own handwriting as "scribbling." In fact, as is evident from this facsimile, Louis's writing was perfectly legible.

Coupvray, 1 September 1831[1]

Sir,
I have the honor of writing these lines to request the renewal of your promise to keep me informed of the date of our next concert.

If I receive no response by Monday, I would ask you kindly to agree to my returning to the Institution on Tuesday. Pardon, Sir, the pestering of your affectionate student.
Louis Braille

I am rather happy, dear Mr. Pignier, that you may have lost only a quarter of an hour in deciphering the first page of this scribble. Do not read the rest if you are in a hurry because, from now on, I write for my [own] pleasure and to answer the kind request you have been good enough to ask of me. I had left Coupvray for a few days when two charming letters arrived. Otherwise my second draft would have crossed with your second letter. All is well here, but only the garden grapes have ripened. At least I have the satisfaction of enjoying beautiful walks. Give my kind regards to Mademoiselle your sister.

I am thinking of you and of... [ellipsis appears in the original]
Louis Braille

TEACHER

After completing his own studies, Louis was named a *répétiteur* (a kind of apprentice teacher) on August 8, 1828.[2] Where previously he slept in a dormitory with all the other students, now Louis was entitled to a room of his own. "If he regretted no longer being able to chat with his friend Gauthier in the evening, he had the peace and quiet necessary for devoting himself to his numerous projects."[3] Louis taught grammar and geography to both blind and sighted students until 1835, after which he taught only blind children in grammar, spelling, geography, history, reading, arithmetic, and algebra.

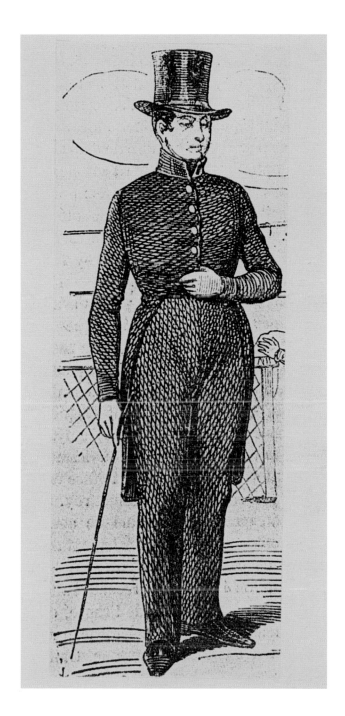

This formal attire, worn by residents of the Quinze-Vingts, is similar to that worn by Louis Braille and his fellow students at the Institute. The lapels on Louis's uniform sported palm leaves — symbols of learning — to show his status as a teacher.

THE 'DEAN'

Braille's standing improved considerably in 1833, when Pignier successfully lobbied Interior Minister Louis Adolphe Thiers[4] to elevate three blind *répétiteurs* to the status of teacher: Louis Braille and his two friends, Gabriel Gauthier and Hippolyte Coltat. The promotion came with a salary of 300 francs a year and the privilege of wearing a uniform that sported silk or gilt palm leaves on both lapels of the jacket.[5] Braille proudly wore his uniform when going to church to play the organ, or whenever he was about town.[6]

Louis was a skillful and popular teacher.[7] According to his friend, Hippolyte Coltat, "He functioned as a teacher with such charm and wisdom that, for his students, the requirement to attend class was transformed into a real pleasure. They competed among themselves, not only to be equal to or better than each other, but to make a sincere and continuous effort to please their teacher, whom they loved as a respected superior and a wise and enlightened friend overflowing with good advice."[8]

Though he could be polite and charming, Braille was no pantywaist. He earned the nickname "dean" (*censeur*) for his willingness to reprimand students who engaged in unbecoming behavior. Where others hesitated to intervene,

Braille would smile and boldly say, "Let's go! I will sacrifice myself."[9] His aim, Coltat informs us, was to make sure that his friends benefited from his "firm and luminous" advice. Coltat further elaborated on Louis Braille's nature:

"His observant mind was at work with such discretion during a conversation, that he wouldn't let anything disagreeable slip out and disturb anyone. He knew how to keep [the conversation] going in an interesting and varied manner. It is said that Labruyère cast off the yoke of one of the greatest difficulties of style — transitions. L. Braille had a natural talent [for them] and made them a permanent study. These chats imperceptibly went from being jocular to earnest and from gracious to harsh in tone. While this was done in a positive manner, he never let it become a society joke [meaning he never let himself become a clown]. He would from time to time show the bright side of his humor and even allowed himself to utter a witty phrase. Some of his expressions became his friends' favorites that soon traveled by word of mouth with the authority and weight of a proverb.

"His words and the tone of his voice were marked by a subtlety that was mirrored on his face, making it difficult to untangle his thoughts from his opinions, as he knew so well how to keep them to himself, thanks to the strength of his character

and his willpower. Once he had made up his mind, he conscientiously did what he had to do, no matter how pleasant or unpleasant; it was enough for him that they were useful. His deportment was controlled by the strictest rules of propriety. He was careful not to let anything slip out that might draw attention to himself. He despised both eccentric and pretentious personalities. His own eccentricity was not to appear eccentric."[10]

> ### LOUIS IS DRAFTED
>
> Louis was conscripted in 1829, and his father accompanied him to the draft board to explain why his son could not serve.
>
> **The Draft Board's records show: "Exempt, being blind at the Hospital of the Quinze-Vingt [sic]." (Braille never lived at the Quinze-Vingts.)**
>
> The Education column, marked with an *O*, meant "cannot read and write." French biographer Jean Roblin remarked, "What a cruel mockery of the man who... endowed blind people with an alphabet!"[11]

A FLAIR FOR DIPLOMACY

Several of Braille's letters demonstrate a flair for diplomacy and a head for business. The one below also suggests that, at times, Braille could be garrulous. Here, Louis speaks on behalf of someone who evidently did not have direct access to Pignier. The gentleman he refers to, Emile Pierre Trencheri, was hired a few months later by Samuel Gridley Howe to teach at the New-England Institution for the Education of the Blind (now Perkins School) in Boston, Massachusetts. Trencheri did very well in the United States, and associated with such luminaries as Longfellow, Emerson, and Prescott, the renowned blind historian. In 1836, Trencheri established the first music store in the Midwest and sold the first piano to be shipped west of the Mississippi. He played the organ in the Roman Catholic cathedral in Alton, Illinois, and continued to tune pianos up to the age of 90.[12]

Coupvray, 20 September 1831

Sir, I shall not have the honor of speaking to you in this letter about Mr. Déchasait to whom I have a thousand obligations. I am writing today for somebody who is unaware of the step I am taking, and to whose interests I cannot be indifferent. The person from whom we were supposed to collect 30 francs for singing has been in Dijon for a few months.

This person must have met with Trencheri either to give him the amount to reimburse him, or to advise him that the money had not been requested. But my friend's silence leads me to believe that Mr. De Ruba has received the requested sum. He never mentioned it, not even in his last letter. That is why I intended to ask Trencheri for a receipt signed by him or by that person. I would have delivered it to you, asking you to append it to the bill that Mr. De Ruba owes to the students. But I have changed my mind: I shall do nothing of the sort. It is more reasonable to entrust you with this matter. Forgive me, Sir, the liberty I took in speaking of something that concerns me only indirectly. However, allow me to tell you with confidence that I would deem myself happy if, having had the honor to communicate my brief to you, I may have the sweet satisfaction that you may come to the same conclusion. Before my departure, I forgot to mention to you Roustant, who could be accepted in a higher grade if you deem it suitable.

Do not tell me: damned talk [maudit parler], be quiet! One more word and I shall end by asking you to admit the new students to the history class.

Please, Sir, accept my mother's, brother's, and my respects. We also beg you to kindly convey our regards to Mademoiselle your sister.

It is my honor to be your very respectful student.
L. Braille

Dr. Pignier must have responded promptly, since Braille mailed another letter only a few days later. It is a pity that none of Pignier's letters have been found. Braille took pains not to abuse his favored position with Pignier when he solicited his counsel on behalf of others. Coltat said of Louis, "When he did [a good deed], he acted with such simplicity and delicacy that he hid, so to speak, the hand of the benefactor from the recipient of his kindness."[13] In the following letter, Braille asks Pignier how a blind friend of his could get the most money possible from his Quinze-Vingts pension when he cashes it in. Beyond Louis's obvious attention to detail, his letters express a penchant for orderliness. This letter is in Louis-Simon's handwriting.

From Coupvray, 2 October 1833

Sir, the kindness you have shown me would have been enough to induce me to return to Paris during my vacation, but I had already decided to come back the day after I wrote to you. I expect to arrive at the Institution on the 9th of this month between nine and ten in the evening. I have a letter from Chauvin in which he asks me to thank you for the box you sent him. It seems that he already received the first three months of the half-pension at the Quinze Vingt[s]. Perhaps this business was not quite clear to you. He told me he had sent me two letters at the Institution but I never received them.

A more embarrassing thing is that the postmaster from his province gave him twenty-eight francs and fourteen sous for the pension, covering the three months to July, when he should have received thirty-seven francs and ten sous. He is asking me what would be the best way for him to get his money. I believe that he should send a certificate of residence four times a year to a Parisian so that the person could cash [his money order] and mail the proceeds to him. I believe that he would then lose only four francs each time, including the postage.

I beg you, Sir, to tell me what your thoughts are on this subject. I hesitate to bother you for a stranger when I know how your children at the lycée[14] take up all your time. However, he was once among your students and is recommended by a person who loves you and dares to hope for the same in return. Please tell my friends about my arrival so that I can find everything in order. I also ask you to share the good news about Chauvin. I dearly hope that Mademoiselle your sister's health will improve.

My mother, myself, and my brother send you and your sister our regards. Sir I have the honor to be your respectful and affectionate student,

Braille Louis

"Pay attention child, you haven't kept me from wandering into a pile of trash." Guided by sighted children, three blind gentlemen, in their distinctive Quinze-Vingts attire, leave the gates of the precinct. Distracted by a friendly dog, one guide allows a blind man to wander into a drunk passed out on the street.

THE LOSS OF A FATHER

Louis Braille was 22 when his father died on May 31, 1831. A despondent Louis-Simon, Louis's brother, bore the burden of giving Louis the sad news and bringing him home from Paris for the funeral. Simon-René's last days had been full of worry about his younger son's future. In a letter written by Louis-Simon, the old *bourrelier* begged the school's director, Dr. Pignier, never to abandon his son. Pignier later wrote that he had already accepted this sacred responsibility "before it was asked."[15]

Handwriting of Louis-Simon, Louis's brother, writing on behalf of their ailing father to Dr. Pignier.

Coupvray, 30 May 1831

Sir, this is in reply to your letter, which I just received, asking for news about our good father. I write in anguish that he is dangerously ill, that he stopped urinating two days ago, and no longer wants to drink wine.[16] It makes us very sad and causes us much pain to hear his constant moaning. Sir, I must tell you that my father thanks you for the good care you have given my brother. Sir, my father entrusts you and Mademoiselle your sister never to abandon him. Sir, you ease my father's bad condition. Sir, my father and my mother send their love as well as my brothers [corrected in the margin to "brother"] and sister. I have the honor to greet you.

[Louis-Simon] Braille

SURROGATE FATHER

The obligation Dr. Pignier willingly accepted affirmed his role as surrogate father to Louis Braille. When Louis-Simon wrote again to Dr. Pignier a few days later, the focus had shifted to Monique Braille, now a widow at age 61. During this period of bereavement, Monique was evidently staying at Louis-Simon's home in Chelles.[17] The affection that she held for her husband of 39 years was evident, but so was her resolve to endure the loss.

Chelles, 3 June 1831

When I had the honor of writing to you on May 29,[18] I didn't want to put off telling you the sad news [about my father] because of the very comforting part you and Mademoiselle your sister played in our family's affliction. I will say that our mother is very distressed, but she has resigned herself to endure this great sorrow. My brother hopes to return to the Institution Monday evening.

I have the honor to greet you. Kindly accept my mother's respects and my brother's affection. We ask you to give our regards to Mademoiselle Pignier.

[Louis-Simon] Braille

LOUIS INHERITS THE BRAILLE HOME

It took more than a decade to settle Simon-René's estate. Louis inherited the family home and a parcel of land. When the Paris-to-Strasbourg railroad was constructed in 1846, Louis arranged to sell his land to the company and wisely invested the proceeds in more land, which his brother farmed.

Simon-René had wanted Louis-Simon to continue the family trade of harness-making, but he lacked his father's patience and taste, and preferred instead to cultivate vines.[19] Two nephews did carry on the trade.

Braille's home in Coupvray.

Louis Braille's father, Simon-René, drew his last breath in the marital bed in an alcove off the kitchen/living room. The window was draped with a dark curtain and the room illuminated with candles.

Louis's grief over his father's death and the decline in his own health were expressed in a letter he wrote to Pignier later that summer. At this date, Louis did not know the nature of his illness, but Pignier, a doctor, might have suspected that the young man's chronic illness was tuberculosis. As Louis's condition deteriorated, Pignier would, from time to time, advise Louis to reduce his teaching load and take a break in Coupvray.

In a letter written in the summer of 1831, Louis struck a note of restlessness at his forced summer respite, wishing he were back at the Institute. The "Academy" to which Braille refers was the illustrious Académie Française, a literary society founded in 1635 by Cardinal Richelieu with the mission of maintaining the purity of the French language. Even as a young man, Braille mingled with *le gratin* (social elite), often attending functions with Pignier.

Lagny, 26 August 1831

*Sir, By writing to you myself, I risk being misunder-
stood, but I beg you [to judge] my sentiments by my
intentions, because I still think now as I did in Paris.
Everything in Coupvray recalls the sad memories that
I cannot escape. My health is no worse than it was at
the Institution but the bad weather doesn't make it
any better. While I am resting, you are absorbed by
preparations for the awards. Had I remained in
Paris, I would have known how my pianos* had fared
in the competition, joined in my friends' activities,
and attended with you the great session of the
Academy. I had intended to do just that, but man
proposes and God disposes. I dare hope, Sir, that you
will honor me with a few lines and tell me about
yourself with whom I can no longer read our favorite
moralist, and about your sister, who wasn't well when
I left Paris. If I dared to request of you to speak of
[undecipherable — his pencil point seems to have
broken] the concert. I also enjoyed so much the good
ladies of the infirmary who are such supporters of
yours.*

*My Mother asked me to present you with her respects.
Please extend them, along with mine, to
Mademoiselle Pignier.*[20]

*I have the honor, Sir, of being your respectful
and affectionate pupil.
Louis Braille*

* "pianos" probably refers to his piano
students

ILL HEALTH

Sickness is a constant theme in Braille's
letters, as it was in his life. In many of the
letters Louis wrote to Pignier, he expressed
more concern about the state of Pignier's
health than of his own. The director and
staff worked in the same unhealthy environment as the students and were exposed
to cholera, trachoma, dysentery, and
tuberculosis — the result of over-crowding,
polluted air, contaminated water, and a
lack of sanitation that were commonplace
in most European cities of the early-19th
century. (Even so, Pignier lived to the
ripe old age of 89.)

Coupvray, 2 October 1831

*Sir, I implore you to believe that it is not indifference
that delayed my answer to your kind invitation by a
few days. I was hoping that my letter would be
delivered by someone who was supposed to bring me a
few things from the Institution, but I just found out
that it was not possible. I thank you for your kindness
in considering the financial matter that I had the
honor of discussing with you in my last letter. Some
people from Paris spoke to me about Monsieur Alar;
they told me that he no longer has a home in Paris. As
for the two or three matters, we could find an
amicable solution, not to say the perfect one. I ask
you if this is possible, and if so, to postpone your
decision until my return.*

*The good Déchasait really touched and taught me
during the trip I was honored to make with him. He
honored me with a seat in his carriage from Lagny to
Chessy. The Bishop of Meaux arrived in Coupvray
the same day I did. The literary question undoubtedly
comes from M.J. and his friend's speech. May I,
without appearing ill mannered, beg you, Sir, to send
me the history grades?*

*Farewell, Sir. Stay healthy for your children's sake,
live before you work: health is a treasure whose value
is recognized only when it is lost. These are old wives'
tales that are still true; it is always glorious to apply to
you the things that you have so often [said to me].
The countryside is my only remedy.*

*I feel well and I hope that this letter finds you the
same, as well as Mademoiselle your sister.
L. Braille*

Coupvray, 11 October 1831

*Sir, It is more than fifteen days since I had the honor
of hearing from you. If I were joking, I would tell you
that I am convinced you wrote to me, and that I must
pick up your letter from the post office. But that is not
what worries me; is the state of your health more
alarming? I can imagine that you are totally
absorbed in certain matters. Shall I still read with you
two of my beautiful [obscured by ink blot...]? These
thoughts each occur to me in turn, but I will candidly
admit that the latter does not seem likely.*

So far, I have spent my vacation amid the vineyards and on the roads but dampness, rains, and winds made me modify my routine. I am being read to, I tune pianos, I play cards and chess, and I feel well. I pray God to protect you as well as Mademoiselle your sister.

Your wholly devoted
L. Braille

Coupvray, 2 January 1832

Sir, I am sorry that I could not be with your children yesterday to express our concerns about your health. I had hoped to be relieved of a social obligation tomorrow, but I cannot get away until the end of the week. Would you please write a note authorizing this delay? It will probably arrive the day before I get back. However, a few words about your health and our Institution would be very precious to me.

Best wishes to you and your sister from my family and my young scribe.[21] The very cold weather here in Coupvray has not impaired my health. I apologize if my colleagues had to put themselves out to find a replacement for me. I will thank them personally when I get back.

I have the honor of being, Sir, your respectful and affectionate student.
Louis Braille

MADEMOISELLE PIGNIER

Louis mentions Pignier's sister in nearly every letter, implying an emotional attachment to her beyond mere courtesy, and indicating that she offered him advice. One letter mentions Mademoiselle's bad teeth, possibly a consequence of her chronic poor health. Even for well-situated people, bad teeth made life miserable — no aspirin to dull the pain, no good fillings, no effective treatment for gum disease. Extraction of a decayed tooth was a very painful procedure (sometimes carried out in the street) but was the best remedy for chronic toothache.

Coupvray, 23 September 1833

Sir, this letter is to say hello and to find out how you and your sister are doing. As for myself I feel great and my arm is healing well but I find it very restricting. I spend my days eating grapes and feeling happy. I am not coming back to Paris before the 23rd of October if I'm not needed before then.

I ask you to let my colleagues know my plans, and I dare hope that you will take some time from your numerous occupations and honor me with a few lines. Is Mademoiselle your sister still suffering from her teeth? Does your young student read well enough?

Did his father give you the last part of his work? I beg you not to search any longer for the story of Joseph because the book I already have will last me until the end of my vacation: I read only when we are fogged in and I spend the remainder of the day in the fields. I also avoid people so as not to speak too much.[22]

Sir, please accept my family's regards and mine in particular to Mademoiselle your sister. I have the honor of being your affectionate student,
Louis Braille

Coupvray, 22 October 1833

Sir, I wish I had been able to give you details of the pleasures of the countryside during beautiful autumn days. This is why I am late in writing to you, but I renounce this claim as it appears that we have only wind, fog, and rain as proven by the clogs that I have been wearing since my return! Despite all that, my health is good, and I hope to spend a pleasant and useful upcoming school year, particularly while benefiting from the kindness of your good sister, who promised to help me in my studies. All bodes well for a satisfying future, especially if my doctor softens the regimen that he has threatened me with. Invite him to do this, dear Sir, I beg you; he is one of your friends. In eight days, I shall be near you who shows me such kindness, at Mademoiselle Pignier's, who knows so well how to ease everything, and amidst my comrades who have proven their friendship so well.

Bodoin is undoubtedly still my equal, alas! Poor boys that we are, we shall not have this happiness. As for me, I do not suffer as much as others from our infirmity, but it is nonetheless significant. Enough of melancholy. With you all will be well.

Your respectful and affectionate student.
L. Braille

Apparently, Louis was something of a celebrity at home, especially for his feats of memory, possibly enhanced by the course in mnemonics he had taken at a local college in 1832. He later taught classes on the subject.[23]

Coupvray, 18 September 1834.

Sir, [being] away from you for a few days, I am worried because I have left you alone in spite of myself, and Mademoiselle your sister might have suffered some setback. Shall I be fortunate enough to have you write me a few lines? I fear that you might not do this right away, but if Mademoiselle Pignier.... The hell with convention... [ellipses appear in the original]. May it be God's will that I receive news from you soon.

Everything in Coupvray is as I predicted. I will return in two weeks. The noblemen and priests in the area have complimented me profusely on what they had read in the family journal. That, as well as my ability to quickly give the dates of moon phases particularly increased my reputation in the region. I give singing lessons on the charming sentimental songs that Roissant has chosen for me with such discerning kindness.

Please give me details on the health of Mademoiselle your sister. Have the missing ones written to you? Everything is probably going well at the Institution except for you, Sir, who are always engrossed in administrative business.

Forgive me, Sir, if I have strained your eyes for so long, and please accept this expression of the sincere attachment and respect of your pupil.
L. Braille

[P.S.] Imposing on your kindness, Sir, I kindly request that you mail the attached notes at the small post office.

Coupvray, 29 September 1834

Sir, you may still be alone. This thought afflicts me; my family and my health must be quite dear to me to make me resist the desire I have to return to Paris. I wish I had been cheerful enough to lighten the burden of your solitude. I will return next Thursday. I hope to see Mademoiselle your sister again, for I like to think that her health has been restored.

Here the great fogs have begun. Soon we shall probably have rain; in this weather no more pleasure.

You might find that I am quite late in writing to you. It is not my fault, although you may not believe it. Well, Sir, speak of me to whomever asks about me and please accept the sentiments with which I have the honor to be your respectful and affectionate pupil.
L. Braille

Coupvray, 1 October 1835

Sir, You are so good to me that you are undoubtedly surprised by the delay in receiving my letter. For others, eight days would be nothing, but for us it is a lot. I would love to settle into an armchair next Saturday and listen to Mademoiselle your sister, who always seeks to please you, read the Golden Bough[24] [Rameau d'or] to me. Would you forward the enclosed letter to Gauthier? A word from you would satisfy both my mind and my heart, but I do not dare request it because it would not find me in Coupvray. May I ask, Sir, that you bring me to the attention of those who are kind enough to remember me.

With regards to Mademoiselle Pignier
Your very respectful student Braille

Too ill to travel far, Louis Braille sometimes played the organ at the nearby Lazarist Church of Saint-Vincent-de-Paul. He felt an affinity for the Lazarists because their founder, Saint-Vincent-de-Paul, once lived in the building on rue Saint-Victor that was later occupied by the school. Braille bequeathed 50 francs to the Lazarists upon his death.

MUSIC

Braille excelled in music from the start of his studies at the Institute, winning the top prize for solo cello in his fifth year. By then, Braille's reputation as a musician was firmly established. An excellent organist, he played in several parishes in Paris, including Notre-Dame-des-Champs and Saint-Nicolas-des-Champs, which had a fine ancient instrument.[2] During summer vacations, he earned pocket change tuning pianos around Coupvray. In 1839, when one of his very capable students was about to leave the Institute with no means of making a living, Louis offered him his own position at Saint-Nicolas-des-Champs.

Musical figurines circa 1837.

A GOOD EAR

The Institute was noted for the high caliber of its music programs, dating back to the time of Guillié. Nonetheless, blind musicians such as Louis were seriously hampered by the lack of a system of musical notation that could be read with the fingers — the same fingers that were needed to play the instrument! Haüy had introduced music to students at the school from the beginning, but his methods shared the same weakness as his raised-print efforts: He simply enlarged and embossed print staves and notes, which proved impossible to read by touch. That left most blind musicians with only two options: either improvise or memorize the piece. "While a good ear is important and improvisation is an excellent talent, a printed score is crucial if a musician, blind or sighted, wishes to adhere strictly to what a composer has written."[3]

It is indeed a challenge to present written music efficiently to the fingers. To use computer terminology, the sense of touch processes information serially (one bit of information after another), but the eye uses parallel processing. At a glance, the eye conveys to the brain a wide variety of musical information arrayed spatially in print: clefs, staves, time and key signatures, fingering, chords, accidentals, and so forth. With one look, the

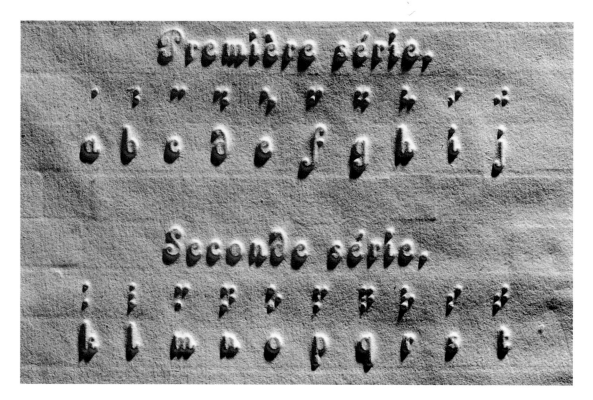

This page from Louis's 1829 publication, "Method of Writing Words, Music and Plain Chant by Means of Dots, for Use by the Blind and Arranged for Them," used both embossed print and dots.

eye can also detect how notes are to be played: staccato, legato, bowed, plucked, muted, softer, louder, faster, slower, and so on. Louis Braille overcame this challenge with his elegant music code that gave the world's blind musicians not only better access to a source of profound pleasure but also opened up precious employment opportunities.

BRAILLE'S SOLUTION

Braille's own students had urged him to find a way to adapt his user-friendly raised-dot system to music.[4] His earliest music code was based on a method devised by 18th-century composer Jean-Jacques Rousseau (1712-1778),[5] which had been adopted by the Institute to replace Haüy's system. Yet Rousseau's music had two very serious defects: It relied on embossed print, and it could not depict the *values* of musical notes.

Braille first improved upon Rousseau's method by replacing Rousseau's hard-to-read embossed print with his own six-dot braille code.[6]

Remarkably, Braille's simple cell handled all aspects of music without ambiguity.

In 1829, the school published Louis's *Method of Writing Words, Music and Plain Chant by Means of Dots, for Use by the Blind and Arranged for Them*, which depicted the musical notes to be sung in braille dots, while the words appeared in embossed print. This innovation, which applied to singing only, was imperfect, and Braille spent five years reworking it. He revamped the music code entirely and based it on the seven notes that form a musical scale in the *Solfège* system (in French, *ut, re, mi…*, in English, *do, re, mi…*,[7] or notes CDEFGAB).[8] In this way, the seven notes in a scale have the same tactile profile in every octave.

Ingeniously, Louis recycled the braille letters *d* through *j* to represent eighth notes in the musical scale. To make them quarter notes, Braille added a dot 6. To make them half notes, he added a dot 3. To get either whole or sixteenth notes, he added both dots 3 and 6. These dots *always* identify the note itself; other dots tell the musician in which octave the notes are to be played (or sung), and other relevant aspects of musical notation.

```
1 · · 4
2 ● · 5
3 ● ● 6
```
Staccato

```
1 ● ● 4
2 · · 5
3 · · 6
```
Slur

BRAILLE MUSICAL NOTES.[13]

Musical Scale	C	D	E	F	G	A	B	
Eighth note:	(braille)	(braille)	(braille)	(braille)	(braille)	(braille)	(braille)	♪
Quarter note:	(braille)	(braille)	(braille)	(braille)	(braille)	(braille)	(braille)	♩
Half note:	(braille)	(braille)	(braille)	(braille)	(braille)	(braille)	(braille)	♩
Whole/16th note:	(braille)	(braille)	(braille)	(braille)	(braille)	(braille)	(braille)	♪

It seems at first confusing that notes on the fourth line can be either whole notes or 16th notes. In fact, the blind musician looks at the values of the other notes in the same measure to determine the value of such a note.[9] To indicate chords, only the fundamental note is written; all other members of the chord are indicated by their intervals from the written note. Octaves are shown "simply by having the notes preceded by a symbol assigned to each octave."[10] Braille's music code is perfectly logical — perhaps more logical than print music, where notes assume many different shapes and have a different appearance depending on the octave in which they appear. This means that a sighted musician has many more notes to learn than a blind musician does.[11]

By 1834, he had developed the basic music code from which has evolved the intricate system now used by blind musicians. Unlike Braille's literary code, which took decades to gain acceptance, his system for musical notation was so superior that it was adopted almost at once. In 1866, a music teacher at the Missouri Institution for the Education of the Blind asserted of Braille's code, "…for music it is impossible to speak of too high praise in regard to it."[12]

Unlike print music, braille music does not appear spatially on a staff. Methods of formatting or arranging braille music on a page vary according to the instrument and also from country to country.[14] In print music, a vertical line separates bars into measures; in braille, measures are separated by a space. Piano and organ music is often presented on a page with the braille measures aligned vertically (one above the other) for each hand. A third set of measures, aligned vertically with the other two, shows organ notes played by the feet, as in print music.

The braille music code is flexible enough to meet the unique requirements of any instrument. In the drum, for example, dots 2-6 indicates a flam, while dots 4-5, followed by dot 2 in the following cell, means a drum roll.[15]

Since the blind musician's hands and ears substitute for the eyes, it would seem nearly impossible to "sight read" a score and play at the same time. Typically, a blind musician memorizes a braille score before performing a piece of music. Some blind musicians are capable of placing both hands on braille piano music, hearing the music in their head, then going directly to the piano and playing it.[16] Blind pianist George Shearing speaks in his biography

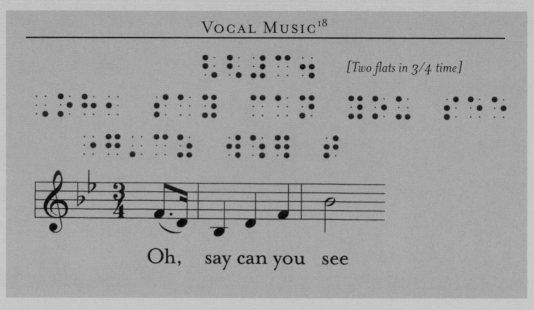

VOCAL MUSIC[18]

[Two flats in 3/4 time]

Oh,   say can you   see

Comparison of braille music and conventionally transcribed music.

about a friend who could "read through a short piece of braille music on a bus on the way home, and play it when he got there."[17] Another form of "sight-reading" involves reading the score with one hand and playing with the other. For choral or solo singing, a blind vocalist can "sight-sing" at least as fast as those who can see — often surpassing them. When taking melodic dictation, blind children can often braille the notes with a slate and stylus faster than their sighted peers can write with a pencil and paper. (Prior to Braille's music code, blind musicians could not write musical notation themselves.) Such is the great gift Louis Braille bequeathed to blind musicians throughout the world.

AN EXCELLENT ORGANIST

In 1832, while still an instructor at the school, Louis contemplated a full-time position as organist of Saint-Etienne's cathedral in Meaux.[20] Coupvray was in the diocese of Meaux where his first teacher, Abbé Palluy, had been a canon since 1826. Perhaps Palluy or Pignier (who had extensive church connections) notified Braille of the opening. Louis may have welcomed the chance to be nearer home, now that his mother was a widow. The details of this possible career change emerge in five letters Braille wrote to Pignier in the fall of 1832.

Lagny, 6 September 1832

Sir, the organist of Meaux died last week. His sister and wife play a little organ, but I don't believe that they can replace him. Please consider Jantier or me, Louis Braille, for the position. I put myself completely in your hands because I am powerless on my own. Sir, please forgive this lack of form.

I respectfully have the honor to be your affectionate and respectful student,
Louis Braille

The chapel at the Institut National des Jeunes Aveugles (INJA) is home to this magnificent organ, which dates back to the building's opening in 1844. Louis Braille probably displayed his "brilliant" playing on this very instrument.[19]

Meaux, 7 September 1832

Sir, I have spoken with the vicar and secretary of the bishop of Meaux. They told me that the position pays 500 francs.[21] They expect the organist to be able to tune the pianos in an 8-league (32 kilometers — 20 miles) radius so the job should really pay 1,500 francs. This man received me very well and took my name. There may be a competitive examination in six weeks. I shall definitely be back at the Institution by next Tuesday. I have the honor to be, Sir, your respectful and affectionate student, Braille.

Meaux, 28 September 1832

Sir, the organist position in Meaux pays only 355 francs, the one to tune pianos [is] at the invitation of Pesuplare in Meaux and there are but a few cathedrals in the area. Following the opinion of my relatives and your good advice, I told Abbé Pelais[22] that I would turn down the offer. I forgot to say that it is very expensive to live in Meaux and I don't believe that I could easily live there as a seminarian. I shall give you the details and answer your excellent letters in a few days. I have the honor of being, Sir, your affectionate student. Louis Braille

Please extend my thanks to Monsignor Ploilue.

Several weeks later, Braille still felt the need to justify his decision not to accept the Meaux position. Dr. Pignier and others had evidently gone to great lengths to help Louis with his application as organist, and Louis thought that his decision not to accept the position might have upset the director. He also felt a little guilty over relaxing during his vacation rather than making money by tuning pianos.

Coupvray, 18 October 1832

Sir, your good letter gave me a lot of satisfaction because I was looking forward to it, and I see that your very busy life doesn't prevent you from thinking of me from time to time. I understand only too well the truth of what you say about Mr. Carton,[23] and I much regret not being able to keep up with last year's correspondence that pleased and honored me so much.

Allow me, Sir, to correct a mistake made by my previous scribe by asking you to tell my friends about the outcome of the Meaux business. It is only fair for them to know since they were the ones who made wishes and sacrifices for my success. People still talk to me about this position and that the main income comes from society balls, making it often necessary for me to sleep in the neighboring castles, in conditions that are not even comparable to being in a seminary, so I have definitely given up the idea of such a position.

I did manage to tune a few pianos and if I had been more enterprising I would have had a lucrative vacation, but I preferred to enjoy the pleasures of the countryside and come back with more zeal for my studies and classes at the end of the month.

Sir, kindly pay my respects to Mademoiselle your sister. Your respectful and affectionate student, Braille

And best regards from my mother and all the family.

THE WELL-TUNED PIANO

The art of piano tuning by those without sight was perfected around 1830, when two blind students at the Institution, one of whom was Claude Montal (1800-1865), tried to tune the piano on which they were practicing. A sighted man who was paid to tune the school's pianos complained to the director, Dr. Alexandre-René Pignier, who ordered the students never to do it again. Undeterred, they got hold of an old piano and practiced taking it apart and putting it back together, until they were satisfied that it was thoroughly repaired and well-tuned. Dr. Pignier watched their labors with interest and decided to put their skills to good use. He asked them to do extensive work on the organ and placed two sighted workmen at their disposal. Montal quickly earned a reputation as one of the best tuners in Paris; he was engaged by professors of the Conservatoire and employed by some of the leading professional musicians. He eventually opened his own piano manufacturing shop.

Meanwhile, piano tuning became the leading profession of graduates of the Institution: some 60 percent of the boys chose music as a career, and about half of these also obtained diplomas in piano-tuning.[24]

Louis Braille could use his talent as an organist to supplement his income, but most blind musicians earned their crust by playing in the streets. The instrument shown here, the hurdy-gurdy, was popular at the time with blind beggars. Its strings vibrate when pressed against a rotating wheel by means of a small keyboard. Because some strings drone constantly, it sounds rather like a bagpipe.

From Coupvray, 30 October [September] 1832

Sir, what distresses me the most is that your efforts as well as those of your friends were useless. It is also because I fear that in the future you will hesitate to recommend others, but you would have thought me very foolish to yield to the vanity of becoming the Meaux organist at whatever cost. This missed opportunity will be more profitable for me than you think at the Institution. I beg you to tell all of this to the excellent Mr. Poilout [or Ploilue] to whom I would write myself if I dared. I forwarded the letters to Mr. Breuil and Mr. Prunaux with the corrections but I kept in my portfolio the one addressed to Mr. Chauvaut, whom I didn't see, as well as the one to my Lord Bishop, who must have come last Friday to the Institution, and all the other letters.

I worry about the first one you wrote me, but I feel that I do not deserve more disgrace. I beg you to tell me if I should come back for Saint Denis's Day. If you have as much trouble replacing me as I have in finding a scribe, that is no small matter.

Please, Sir, convey my respects to Mademoiselle your sister, who has given me such good advice, and speak of this matter to my colleagues. With these thoughts in mind, I have the honor of being always your respectful and affectionate student, Louis Jean Philippe Braille.[25]

Please also accept the thanks of my mother and all our family. Signed LB

THE NEXT CHALLENGE

As the letters in this chapter show, Louis Braille was one of a select group: a literate blind man at ease communicating with the sighted world in 19th-century France.

But Braille was a perfectionist; he could never be certain his "scribbling" was legible or that the scribe to whom he dictated a letter was literate. He understood all too well the difficulties faced by his "fellows in misfortune," many of whom never mastered cursive writing techniques and were thus deprived of a means of communicating with families and friends. With characteristic determination, Louis now set out to solve the problem of writing to those who could see.

Students posed outside the Institute write by means of a raphigraphe, a dot-matrix printer invented by Louis Braille and his friend Pierre-François-Victor Foucault. The device produced documents in print that sighted people could read.

DOT-MATRIX PRINTING

Students at the school for the blind remained away from home much of the year — some too poor even to go home for vacations. Letter-writing was the sole means of staying in touch with family and friends. But writing techniques at the school had not changed since the time of Haüy. Dictating a letter to a scribe had serious drawbacks. Beyond the obvious one of privacy, it was difficult to find scribes. Worse, the scarcely literate scribes wrote phonetically, putting down on paper what they thought they heard, resulting in run-on words and idiosyncratic spelling.[2] Some of the handwriting was atrocious. Moreover, the dependency on scribes, the lack of a practical method that blind individuals could use to write to those who were sighted, was precisely the kind of social barrier Haüy had been determined to overcome all those years ago.

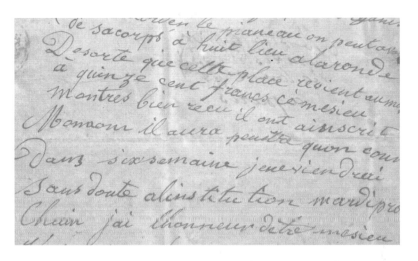

The letters Louis Braille dictated to a scribe were not easy to read.

ABILITY TO WRITE

Braille resolved to find a remedy: "To give blind people the ability to write, to allow them to surmount this obstacle that so markedly restricts their social relations, is an enterprise attempted by those who have occupied themselves with their education; it is a subject that should have been proposed for a prize by the various betterment societies; people will perhaps find I have made a contribution to solving this problem.

"You sometimes see blind people writing with the help of a more or less complicated apparatus, but these are only praiseworthy exceptions that attest to the power of skill united with intelligence…. These privileged blind people cannot read their [own] writing, nor can they even be certain that their pencil or carbon paper have made [dark enough marks]."[3]

In approaching the problem, it helped that Louis had a good grasp of spatial relations, which was reinforced whenever he wrote a letter or note by hand. With characteristic analytical skill, he deduced that all print letters were basically square at the center — a shape that could be represented tactually by four raised dots. Ascenders and descenders, e.g., those on an h or a g that made up the remainder of the letter, could be depicted by three dots embossed vertically above or below the square. In his own words, "To form letters, I have observed that, allowing four dots to form the body of each letter, three dots are needed to form the top or bottom stems; so that the entire height of the letter requires vertical space for ten dots, to be used or not, depending on whether a certain letter requires that space or not."[4] Braille called his system decapoint (ten-dot) because it used a 10x10 dot matrix (though in practice it could be up to 12 dots wide, for the letters M and W and for diphthongs).

TEN-DOT WRITING

Decapoint enabled blind people not only to write to sighted people but also to review the document themselves. (Sighted people could also use this technique to write to those who were blind.)[5] It was written by using a stylus with a rounded tip to press into a sheet of paper only those dots in the matrix that would form the outline of a print letter. A wooden or metal board with openings the same dimensions as a 10x10 matrix was placed

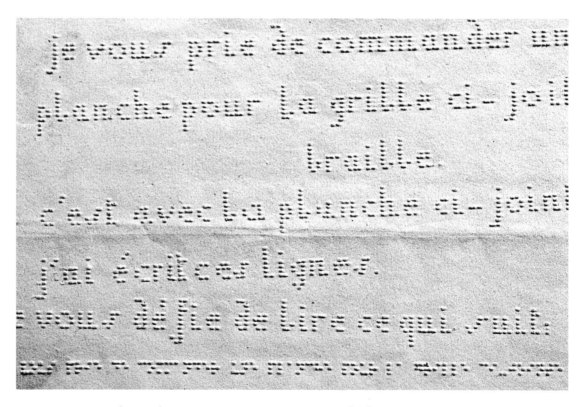

Using his decapoint (ten-dot) method, Braille writes: "Please send [me] a board for the attached grid, braille." [He has left the letter n out of the word jointe.] "I wrote these lines with the attached grid. I defy you to read what follows." In braille, he then writes, "Please send me a board for the attached grid."

over a sheet of paper, which rested on a board with a soft covering, such as leather or flannel, to provide "give." As each opening was used to make a print letter, a grid or mesh with 100 fine openings (formed by wires soldered at right angles) was placed over it. Through these openings, the writer pressed a stylus into the paper to emboss dots to form the shape of a letter of the alphabet. If necessary, the writer could ascertain which dots had to be pressed into the paper by consulting the table Louis Braille had prepared in embossed print.

To be able to produce enough force to dent the paper, dots had to be pressed from the back and so were written in mirror image. The writer made the first line of dots at the right and worked toward the left. When the sheet was turned over for reading, the first character would then be at the left, as in ordinary print. In fact, Louis had conceived what we would now call dot-matrix printing, and he did it with no visual memory of print. This was a singular achievement for a young blind man, especially one debilitated by tuberculosis.

GRIDS & BOARDS

Alexandre Fournier, a former student at the Institute, had traveled to Russia with Haüy back in 1806. He returned to Paris

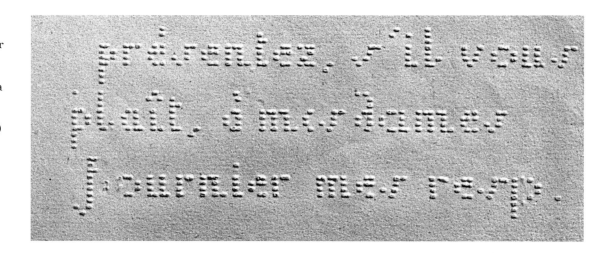

Braille collaborated with Alexandre Fournier to produce grids for his decapoint system that allowed communication between the blind and the sighted. Embossed dots in the form of print letters enabled Fournier, who was blind, and "his ladies," who presumably were sighted, to read Louis's closing regards, "Please give my respects to the Fournier ladies...."

in 1817 and took up residence at the Quinze-Vingts, where he ran the print shop. We know from three extant letters that Louis wrote to Fournier that he helped to supply the grids that Louis needed for his decapoint system. (No grids for writing decapoint are known to have survived.)

In one letter to Fournier, Braille complains that the grids he supplied produce lines that are too far apart, "Perfection and prompt possession is the ardent desire of your friend braille." Fournier must have rectified the situation since Louis writes back enthusiastically, "Here are the new results. I wrote these lines with the grid I supplied you [Louis must have meant that he himself supplied the specifications for the grid]. Can you believe that I wrote these lines with the same grid?" The actual decapoint letter shows that the last three lines are much easier to read — even clearly showing the accent on the word même.

In a third undated letter Braille points out that a cabinet-maker (a skilled artisan, possibly blind) is having difficulties, most likely in meeting Louis's specifications for the job. "The cabinet-maker believes it is so difficult. The ten lines of each opening must take up a quarter less space. Well, send me what he has made, and I will make a modified grid out of it. It will make a perfect board."

RAPHIGRAPHE

Despite the breakthrough Louis made with decapoint, the process remained slow and arduous, and only a few words would fit on a page. Louis had long been aware of the need to conserve space in writing techniques used by blind people, once remarking that for this reason he wanted his sentences to have "more meaning than words."[6]

Fortunately, Braille knew a brilliant mechanic, Pierre-François-Victor Foucault (1797-1871), who had been a student at the Royal Institution for Blind Youth until the year before Louis was admitted. He devised a machine, later known as the raphigraphe (needle-writer), which mechanized and miniaturized Braille's new method for writing print. It was awarded a platinum medal by the Society for the Encouragement of National Industry in 1843.[7]

Biographers of Thérèse-Adèle Husson, Foucault's first wife, who was blind, suggest that Foucault felt impelled to improve writing techniques because he knew firsthand how difficult it was for his wife to put her words on paper[8] (see sidebar).

Facing page:
Louis Braille's friend, François Foucault, helped support his family by playing at the "Café of the Blind," located in the basement of the Palais Royal, where people of all backgrounds gathered for a good time while being entertained by an orchestra of blind musicians. Such was the Café's unsavory reputation that Quinze-Vingts officials tried (in vain) to stop blind residents from going there.

A BLIND COUPLE IN POST-REVOLUTIONARY FRANCE

Thérèse-Adèle Husson (1803-1831) lost her sight to smallpox at nine months of age in Nancy, France. In her early twenties, she decided to move to Paris to earn a living as a novelist, a remarkably adventurous proposition for a woman in post-Revolutionary France. Husson persevered, writing novels and short collections of children's stories, all grounded in the Roman Catholic morals of her day. *The Converted Jewess* (1827) and *Story of a Pious Heiress* (1828), for example, urged both Jews and Protestants to convert to the Roman Catholic faith.[9]

In "Reflections on the Physical and Moral Condition of the Blind," she counsels against marriage between two blind people, yet in 1826 she married a struggling blind musician, Pierre-François-Victor Foucault. Their numerous desperate appeals to the Quinze-Vingts for lodging and financial assistance were rejected (perhaps because of its policy against married couples who were both blind), and they lived in abject poverty. Thérèse died of burns from a fire in their slum apartment in 1831. Such accidents were not uncommon at that time, when coal- or wood-burning stoves were used for heating and cooking.

The following year, Foucault married a seamstress (his second wife was sighted), and they were admitted to the Quinze-Vingts. (There is no record of the fate of his two daughters.) The couple managed a small grocery store on the grounds, and François continued to supplement his earnings as a horn player at the notorious Café des Aveugles. With some newfound stability in his life, Foucault could return to his passion for mechanics, and work with Louis Braille on the invention of the raphigraphe.

Caricature Parisienne.

Café des Aveugles.

Precise Construction

Simple in concept, the raphigraphe required instrument-quality precision in its construction: It had ten pistons arranged like a fan so that they converged to produce a vertical line of dots as high as ordinary print. The fingers of the right hand pushed down a piston that pressed a rod with a sharp point against the paper, where it made a tiny hole or a carbon copy of a dot. The fan-shaped array was mounted on a fine screw thread that carried it horizontally across a page, from margin to margin, under the precise control of a crank turned by the user's left hand. One half turn of the crank positioned the piston-fan to produce the dots specified for the next column; a full turn positioned the array to begin the next print letter; two and one-half turns moved it to the next word.[10] At each position, the necessary pistons could be pressed down, one at a time, to produce a pinprick in the paper, or a dot on a carbon copy. A spring automatically returned the piston to its initial position.

Braille humbly credited Foucault with this invention — which was accurate in the sense that he constructed the mechanical system[11] — but Foucault acknowledged his debt to Braille: "Monsieur Braille, one of the most distinguished teachers at the Institution for Blind Youth,

First Dot-Matrix Printer

The raphigraphe (circa 1840) was the first dot-matrix printer ever made. Louis Braille wrote what we would now call the software for this printer (how to generate letter shapes), and his blind friend, Pierre-François-Victor Foucault, a skilled mechanic, designed the award-winning hardware.

It is possible that Foucault's musical knowledge inspired its design. He had received an excellent musical education under Guillié. As a horn player, and member of the orchestra at the disreputable Café des Aveugles, he was familiar with trumpets. Until the early 19th century, the pitch of a trumpet could be changed only by adding a different length of tubing, called a "crook." In 1815, piston valves were invented to produce this effect instantaneously. The pistons on Foucault's raphigraphe bear a distinct resemblance to the spring-loaded valves of a trumpet!

conceived of the idea of perforated letters well before me. My new machine is nothing but the continuation of his discovery. The handbook [showing which dots to use to represent specific letters] that I use is also his."[12]

The year before Braille's death, Foucault traveled to London to demonstrate his "Printing-Key Frame" at the Great Exhibition of 1851.[13] An eyewitness account of his impressive demonstration in the spectacular Crystal Palace has survived: "The operation of this Printing-Key Frame[14] was witnessed by thousands in the Great Exhibition in Hyde Park, where it also gained a prize medal.[15] The inventor, M. Foucault, was himself the exhibitor, and formed an interesting specimen of talent, perseverance, and ingenuity, under the most discouraging circumstances. M. Foucault is a pensioner at the Quinze Vingt [sic], an establishment for the blind in Paris; but by exerting his musical talents, and by keeping a small shop, in which he is assisted by his wife [Foucault had remarried], he has earned the means of pursuing, at his own expense, those experiments and inventions by which he so zealously endeavours to benefit the blind. During nearly the whole of his stay in England, at the time of the Great Exhibition, he was bearing his own expenses, and diligently working away with his Printing Frame, and explaining

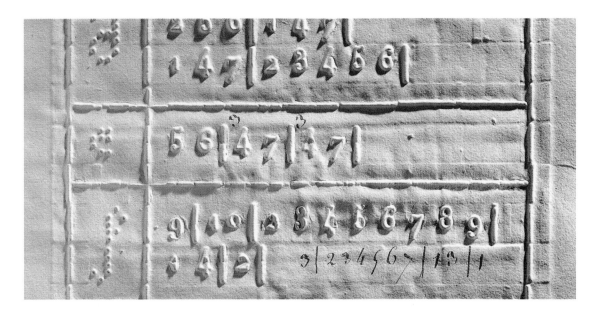

Louis Braille prepared this book to show blind writers which dots had to be embossed in paper to generate a specific letter of the alphabet. (Note the handwritten correction.)

its use and mode of working to little groups of persons in the Crystal Palace, who gathered round him, often without any knowledge of the language in which he so eloquently addressed them, but from curiosity to see a blind person using with much rapidity this novel kind of printing machine."[16]

Until the appearance of a practical typewriter in 1867,[17] the raphigraphe was the most user-friendly piece of equipment available to blind people who wanted to write to those who could see. It is a largely forgotten product of Braille's genius. Ironically, it was a young blind man who first invented a means of representing visual information by means of

dots in a matrix. Louis Braille used only 100 dots at most, but employed the same principle as do modern electronic devices — television screens, computer displays, digital cameras, cell phones — though they use millions of dots, or pixels.

RAPHIGRAPHE LETTERS

Several letters Louis Braille wrote by raphigraphe have survived, and are as readable today as when they were written. In the following letter Braille wrote to the jovial and influential Abbé Charles Carton of Bruges, Belgium, director of the Institute for Deaf-Mutes and the Blind, in hopes that the Abbé would find the raphigraphe useful for his students.[18]

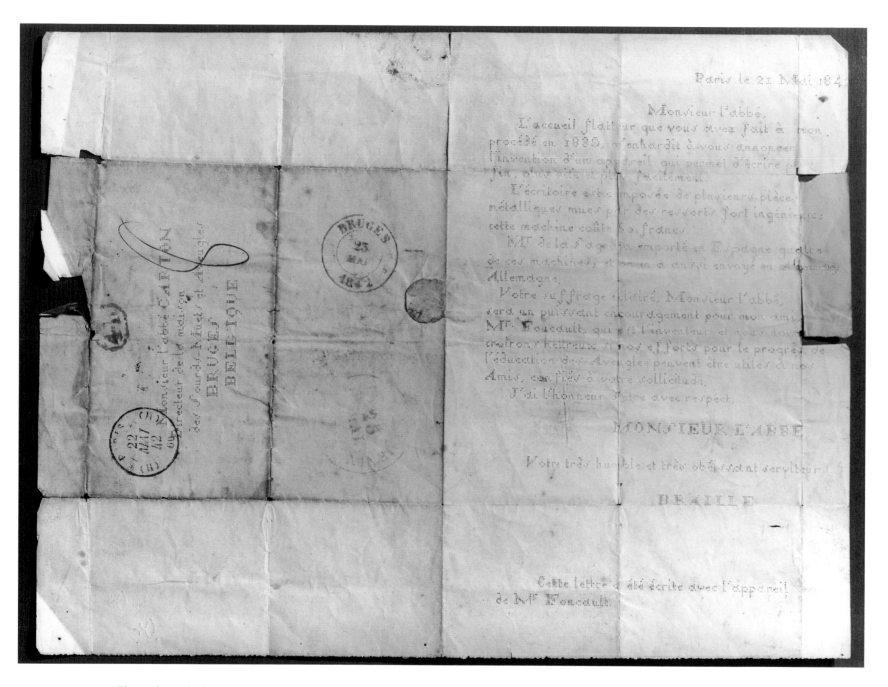

This raphigraphe letter was written to the influential Abbé Charles Carton, director of the Institute for Deaf-Mutes and the Blind, in Bruges, Belgium. The print letters were formed by pinpricks in the paper, which allowed a blind person to read back what he or she had written. Later versions of the raphigraphe did not have this feature, but used carbon paper to give a better image of the print.

Paris, 21 May 1842

Monsieur l'Abbé, The flattering welcome you gave to my procedure in 1839, emboldens me to let you know about a new apparatus that allows people to write more clearly, more quickly, and more easily. The writer is composed of several pieces of metal moved most ingeniously by springs: this machine costs 50 francs. Mr. de la Sagra[19] has imported four of these machines to Spain, and one of them has also been sent to Germany. Your clear approval, Monsieur l'Abbé, will give strong encouragement to my friend Mr. Foucault, who is the inventor, and we would consider ourselves happy if our efforts on behalf of the educational progress of the blind could be useful to our friends confided to your care. I have the honor to be with respect your very humble and very obedient servant.

BRAILLE
[P.S.] This letter was written with Mr. Foucault's apparatus.

Two raphigraphe letters to Pignier confirm Louis's involvement with the upper reaches of Parisian society. Louis mentions a reception for Mr. Etienne-Denis Pasquier, who had become Chancellor of France in 1837 and a duke in 1844. He had been Prefect of Police in Paris under Napoleon and was a respected member of his Council of State. On February 17, 1842, Pasquier was elected to the Academy and Louis was anxious to attend the reception for him.[20]

Paris, 14 June 1842

Sir, I have the honor of writing you these lines for different purposes. First, I will tell you that Monsieur Colbert lives at rue Meslée No. 9. [9 is written as a mirror image, and Braille seems to catch his mistake for he immediately writes the word neuf (nine).] Your protégé would accept with pleasure his chances in a competitive exam. I am still thinking about the reception for Monsieur Pasquier if there is still time.

Your affectionate
Braille

Paris, 2 November 1842

Sir, I have just learned that the reception for Monsieur Pasquier will take place on Thursday, the eighth of this month. I am afraid that your work, your health, and the bad weather and, above all, the delay, will not allow you to obtain two tickets for me.

However, if against all hope you can satisfy my wishes, I beg you to send the tickets by messenger.[21] Forgive, Sir, such a brief letter, but the bell[22] has sounded for class.

Respect and gratitude to you and Mademoiselle, your sister.
Braille

Louis accompanied Pignier to numerous soirées, where it was not uncommon for Louis to be asked to perform on the piano. Despite the accolades he received for his "brilliant" playing, Louis did not enjoy being the center of attention — an attention he felt was often tinged with pity. At the end of the evening, he would be guided home by Miss Pignier... and joyfully regained the solitude of his own room.[23]

The following raphigraphe letter, written one year before Louis's death, confirms the lifelong friendship he and Pignier enjoyed during their twenty years of correspondence. It was written a decade after Pignier had been forced out of the Institute and speaks of Louis's continued affection.

Paris, 25 February 1851

Sir, Since I was not able to stop by your home last Sunday, I have the honor of announcing to you that Coltat and I will visit [visite spelled vste] next Thursday. We would be delighted [to be] with you and Mademoiselle, your respected and good sister. These are always the sentiments of your totally devoted children,
Coltat, Braille

Two of three enormous volumes of A Brief History of France, *which in 1837 was the first full-length book to be brailled using Louis's code.*[1]
Deputy Director Pierre–Armand Dufau used this pioneering book in his campaign to oust Dr. Pignier.

"When a true genius appears in the world, you may know him by this sign: that all the dunces are in confederacy against him."

Jonathan Swift (1667-1745)

BRAILLE BANNED

In 1840 Louis Braille experienced a terrible setback: His mentor and friend, Dr. Pignier, was forced to retire following the machinations of his deputy, Pierre-Armand Dufau. The conflict between the two men reflected the tensions between church and state that persisted long after the French Revolution. Before 1789, the influence of the Roman Catholic Church went far beyond worship and morality. Its land ownership, dominance of education, support of the monarchy, and power to approve or disapprove what could be published were all sources of fierce controversy from one regime to another. Indeed, influential people took it for granted that the state would enforce the policies of the church.

Through the Civil Constitution of the Clergy (1790) and related measures, the French Revolutionary governments confiscated church lands, excluded Catholicism from the educational system, and made the clergy virtual employees of the state. The church partially recovered its privileges under Napoleon in 1802 and under the restored Bourbon Kings Louis XVIII and Charles X in the 1820s. Nevertheless, the heated dispute between the clerical and anti-clerical forces in French society persisted, intruding even upon the Institution at which the pious Louis Braille was a distinguished teacher.

MACHINATIONS OF DUFAU

Pierre-Armand Dufau (1795-1877) joined the Institution in 1815, five years before Dr. Pignier's arrival, and subsequently served as his deputy director.[2] Although Pignier's achievements were such that he was later dubbed the second founder of the school,[3] Dufau was not impressed with his boss. A republican (Girondist), Dufau viewed Pignier as a reactionary, a supporter of the church, and even a monarchist. Dufau even frowned on Pignier's encouraging musically talented students to play the organ, for such employment took students into churches, which he regarded as bastions of superstition, reaction, and privilege. Besides, there was a practical consideration: Close to fifty, intelligent, and ambitious, Dufau realized he would never become director if Pignier were not removed from his post.[4] Furthermore, Dufau's own star was rising: In 1837, his book *The Blind: Considerations on Their Physical, Moral and Intellectual State, with a Complete Description of the Means Suitable to Improve Their Lot Using Instruction and Work* won a prestigious prize from the Académie Française. (The year before, this prize went to Alexis de Tocqueville for his famous book *Democracy in America*.)

Dr. Pignier did indeed represent a world that had supposedly been cast aside by the revolution. His successors would reproach him for running the school more as a seminary than as a college. These very values probably cemented the avuncular relationship between Pignier and Braille, for Braille's father had a similar temperament. Pignier once said of Simon-René Braille, "His integrity and habits bring to mind the old days."[5]

While Dufau's "low intrigues"[6] subjected Pignier to shabby treatment, the criticisms were not entirely unfounded. When Samuel Gridley Howe visited the school in the early 1830s, after Pignier had been director for ten years, he inquired about any educational innovations the school had made since Haüy. There were none. Howe's suggestions for simple modifications to print and maps were met with "… if any improvements could have been made, such great and good men as the Abbé [sic] Haüy and his successors would not have overlooked them."[7]

Howe went so far as to proclaim that the Institution was pervaded by "a spirit of illiberality, of mysticism, amounting almost to charlatanism, that ill accords with the well-known liberality of most French Institutions."[8] Students who wished to learn English, Howe reported, had to do so in secret because "those having the direction of the establishment

had in their wisdom discovered that it was improper for the blind."[9] Evidently, no one told Howe about the reading and writing system recently invented by one of their young students, Louis Braille.

DUFAU PREVAILS

Whatever his motives, Dufau's attitude to Pignier ran close to enmity,[10] and he began a whispering campaign against the director. He noted that Pignier had embossed many books of a religious nature (among them *The Lord's Prayer* in several languages)[11] and some history books that might expose students to counter-revolutionary ideas. As ammunition, Dufau used the very first full-length book to be produced using Louis's braille code, *A Brief History of France*, which had been written by priests, who were identified only by their initials.[12] Eventually, Dufau won over the politicians who mattered. On May 7, 1840, Pignier was forced to retire, and Dufau was made the new director. In this squalid process, Louis lost a valued friend and zealous advocate for his raised-dot code.

The timing of Pignier's dismissal was especially cruel because it prevented him from enjoying the fruits of decades of labor on behalf of his students — a new building. Since his arrival at the Institution in 1821, Pignier had constantly badgered authorities to provide a new

Samuel Gridley Howe had fought as a soldier for Greek independence just before his visit to the Royal Institution for Blind Youth, where he was conducting research for his own school in America. His forceful, outspoken manner may have seemed brash to the rather proper staff at the Institution, who responded to his inquiries with "secrecy and reserve."[13]

facility to replace the unhealthy, tumble-down structure on rue Saint-Victor. At last, on May 14, 1838, an eloquent and impassioned plea by the poet-politician Alphonse Lamartine moved the Chamber of Deputies to allocate funds for a new building. The foundation stone was laid June 29, 1839. Less than a year later, Pignier was ousted, and would not be present at the opening ceremony in 1844.

DUFAU BANS BRAILLE

Once Pignier was out of the picture, the ambitious new director was free at last to implement his own way of doing things. Dufau revised the embossed type introduced by Haüy some fifty-six years earlier to more closely resemble the embossed types being used in Scotland and the United States (e.g., Boston Line Type). These types were only marginally better than Haüy's, but Dufau's position had scientific backing. In 1836, Ramon de la Sagra, a Spanish philanthropist, had

published statistics comparing embossed print used by blind people in the United States with that used in France. These findings showed that the American versions took up less space, used less paper, weighed less, and that the angular shapes used in embossed print developed by James Gall, a blind man in Edinburgh, were easier to read.[14] Such evidence supported Dafau's policies. To ensure that there would be no return to the old ways, Dufau ordered the burning of all books embossed by Haüy's methods — 26 titles produced under Guillié and 47 under Pignier.[15]

Dufau went further still and forbade the use of braille. Like Haüy, Dufau held fast to the view that blind people should use the same reading and writing techniques as those with eyesight in order to avoid erecting barriers between the two. Dufau had also invented a handguide that he believed would facilitate the writing of embossed print, an invention that would be useless if braille were to become the official literacy system.[16] The deputy-director's hostility to Pignier probably carried over to his protégé, Louis Braille, who was also a devout Roman Catholic, *and* he played the organ!

Ultimately, Dufau was not successful. He could ban braille books, he could forbid the act of reading and writing in braille, but he could neither stop the

By November 1843, classrooms were ready for use in the newly constructed building for the Royal Institution for Blind Youth (today the Institut National des Jeunes Aveugles or INJA). That month, a sad procession made its way along rue Saint-Victor: The students and teachers were decamping from the damp, ill-ventilated, unhealthy structure that had been their home-away-from-home for twenty-five years. Their move into a handsome new structure felt almost as if they were heading into exile from an impoverished but beloved land.[17]

students from using it, nor could he force them to return to the old ways. In any case, the blind youngsters felt no love for this solemn and disagreeable man and were not inclined to respect him or his rules.[18] The students knew, from personal experience, that braille was superior to other reading and writing systems; they continued to teach it to each other and, some have claimed, to use it secretly.[19] So eager were they to read braille that they tore pages from *A Brief History of France*. In class, they took notes in braille and compiled them into little exercise books.[20] As one student claimed later, "We had to learn the alphabet in secret, and when we were caught using it, we were punished."[21] (Dufau's ban never applied to music braille, which continued to be used in hybrid books: words embossed in print and musical notes embossed in braille.)[22]

BRAILLE REACHES OUT

A few weeks after Pignier's dismissal, Louis wrote the following letter to the distinguished Viennese educator Johann Wilhelm Klein.[23] The timing might have been coincidental, but it is possible that after Braille had lost his most influential backer, he felt that he should take greater initiative in promoting his ideas. This letter tried to interest Klein in the decapoint method that gives blind people a means of writing to those who can see

(see "Dot-Matrix Printing"). It was not an attempt to promote braille. In any case Louis would not have succeeded in persuading Klein of his code's value. Despite being an enlightened educator and founder of the school for the blind in Vienna in 1804 (the second in Europe), like most sighted people, Klein believed that blind people should use reading and writing methods similar to those used by the sighted. He favored a "needle-stamp" method of reading and writing print that he had invented.[24]

Paris, 11 July 1840

Dear Mr. Klein,
Knowing the keen interest you take in the education of the blind, I have the honor of offering you an explanation of a new way of writing for use by the blind, and I beg you to consider these lines a sincere tribute to your devotion to the unfortunate ones whose fate I share.

I would be happy if my little method could be useful to your pupils, and if this specimen were to be proof for you of the profound devotion with which I have the honor of being,

Sir, your respectful and very humble servant.
Braille
Royal Institution for Blind Youth

Klein was among a small network of talented and capable individuals, such as Samuel Gridley Howe, working in the specialized field of the education of the blind in mid-19th-century Europe. Generally, they tried to keep in touch and learn from one another, as Howe's fact finding visit to various European cities shows. Johann Klein, an avid researcher and prolific writer, was involved in setting Austrian government policy regarding education and may have been behind the unusual request Louis Braille received to tutor a blind prince in the Austrian royal family around this time. Louis declined. According to his family, he asserted, "I am not the servant of only one blind person; I am the servant of all blind people."[25] Such an unusually bold statement from Louis suggests that he had reached an age and a stage in his development where he knew that his contributions did indeed extend to all blind people.

BRAILLE CODE PREVAILS

Dufau's prohibition of braille did not last long. As soon as he became director, he hired his friend, Joseph Guadet, as his deputy. Scion of a distinguished Girondist family, Guadet already had a reputation as a writer and erudite man.[26] He knew nothing about the education of the blind but was open-minded. He could not fail to notice the determination of the students to continue to use braille despite Dufau's ban, and he soon realized that braille was indeed more practical than embossed print. Guadet evidently convinced Dufau that this was the case. Dufau could not publicly admit that he had changed his mind about the usefulness of braille, so he allowed Guadet to sing its praises.

On February 22, 1844, during the inaugural ceremonies of the new building, Guadet read aloud from his 15-page booklet titled *An Account of the System of Writing in Raised Dots for Use by the Blind*, which described the defects in the Barbier system and the superiority of Louis Braille's code.[27] In an exercise reminiscent of Haüy's showing off his students' skills before the royal family in 1786, Guadet followed his "Account" with an experiment. A teacher asked a blind girl to write down some verses of poetry in braille, dictated to her by a member of the audience. These lines were then read out loud by another girl, who had previously been asked to leave the room. Next Guadet had one of the teachers write down a musical phrase dictated by someone else, which was easily read by a young blind student who had been absent from the room.[28]

Louis Braille, and his mother and brother, who were seated in the audience, must have been deeply gratified by the recognition Louis had finally gained after all those years of effort. Guadet said later, "Braille was modest, too modest.... Those around him did not appreciate him, or at least were wrong to leave him in the shade. We were perhaps the first to give him his proper place in the eyes of the public, either in spreading his system more widely in our musical instruction or in making known the full significance of his invention."[29]

The first edition of Dufau's *Des aveugles* (Concerning the Blind), in 1837, scarcely mentioned Braille's code, but the 1850 edition faintly praised Louis's system: "... this system does not make any great philosophical [scientific] claims... nevertheless one can say, it opened up a new era in the education of those deprived of eyesight.... These days at the Institution we tend to freely use the system of M. Braille and make it the true basis of education...."[30] Dufau also admitted that the importance of using print that sighted people could read had been exaggerated.[31]

ILL HEALTH
Louis Braille's health had become fragile while he was still a teenager, but his illness was not identified until 1835, when, at the age of 26, he coughed up blood. The diagnosis was unavoidable — he had tuberculosis. This incurable disease slowly eroded his very sinews. Louis Braille received expert care, but medical skill at that time had little to offer. Two letters — one written in 1831 and another in 1844 — show the marked change in Louis's health. Louis seldom spoke of his personal appearance, but in a letter written before the disease had ravaged his body, he described himself as "neither fat nor slim, rather slim than big."

Coupvray, 25 October 1831

Sir, you have no doubt learned that I intended to return to the Institution at the end of the month, but I did not know for sure until yesterday. I therefore hope, Sir, to visit you on Monday evening. You will not find me a "Samson" but you will find a man neither fat nor slim, rather slim than big, and enjoying satisfactory health, thanks to your more than kindly solicitude. Please accept the wishes that my family and I address to you and Mademoiselle your sister.

L. Braille

"BECAUSE THE SUN THAT RIPENS THE GRAPES MADE ME FORGET...." [LOUIS'S LETTER FROM CHAMALIÉRES]

[P.S.] I have just heard of Monsieur Velvincourt's death. I do not approve the policy or indifference that would not include his name in our public prayers. The receipt of your epistle makes me unfold[32] my letter in order to deny absolutely what you attribute to me. I do not know if I may without objection beg you to write a few more lines, not of satisfaction but of consolation.

By the fall of 1844, Louis's health had deteriorated to the point where he was forced to take a long break in Chamalières.[33] From there, he wrote his longest surviving letter. It shows him making the best of a vacation in the countryside, but the letter is tinged with melancholy. Louis knows that he will not recover from his chronic illness, and is worried about the "new order of things" under Pierre-Armand Dufau, back at the Institution.

Chamalières, 11 October 1844

Sir, During the month of September, I loved to write to my happy friends of the boulevard [site of the new school at 56 Boulevard des Invalides] because the sun that ripens the grapes made me forget the sad thoughts that have preoccupied me for several months. But today, the approach of winter and the new order of things that will begin for me in Paris are the subjects for reflection that cloud over my horizon and rally my feelings for you and Mademoiselle your sister, which I have always found in my painful moments, even more than in prosperous times.

Your children in Chamalières, for you have two here until the middle of next week, were upset to hear about your new sprain, but our friend Coltat reassured us by saying that this accident had had no aftereffects.

No one has told me anything about the health of Miss Pignier. However, she undoubtedly fears the approach of winter, and one of my most ardent wishes is that the bad weather will not prevent me from coming to spend afternoons near her, and the pleasure will be complete because you will be there, especially in the evenings.

I have had no news of my poor mother for two months, which makes me suffer even more, and I plan to take the coach to Lagny, when I get off the one going to Bourges, for I have always intended to spend a few hours in the latter town, if all the stagecoach connections are easy.

I have not spoken to you about my health because I am afraid that the remarkable improvement gained does not wish to accompany me beyond the Orléans Gate [an entrance into Paris]; besides the improvement hangs by a thread, and as I often say, it is the bark that has improved, not the tree itself.

Forgive, Sir, the mixture of joyful and sad ideas, which would displease anyone but you; if I upset you with the sad details, I think you will be pleased by what I have left to tell you about my stay in the countryside. We perform duets and trios, piano, voice, and cello, which electrify the neighborhood. We are happy with this modest audience, and I have absolutely refused any musical get-together in Clermont, despite the fact that my name appeared in a local leaflet in connection with pompous praise meant for someone else.

Don't think, however, that I make music all day long. We keep ourselves busy with it only when the weather is bad, which is rare in September. But, at the moment, cold penetrates our secluded residence and rain often confines me to my pretty little room where, nevertheless, time passes quickly because I am surrounded by care, respect, and I dare say it, affection.

Kindly accept, Sir, the homage of respect and affection that all the family and I offer to you and your sister,

Your affectionate student,
Braille

[P.S.] Will you kindly put the enclosed letter in the mail? I ask Miss Pignier to give my regards to her cordon bleu cook, Miss Louise, whom I hope to see in good health again.

RAVAGED BY TUBERCULOSIS

Novelist Emile Zola vividly described the symptoms of tuberculosis in his novel *Lourdes*. One of the sick passengers on a special train to Lourdes, where they hoped for a miracle cure, is Mademoiselle Grivotte, a woman in her thirties, with a "round, ravaged face." She describes her frightening disease to the other ailing passengers:

"'The doctors say that I have one lung done for, and that the other one is scarcely any better. There are great big holes you know. At first I only felt bad between the shoulders and spat up some froth. But then I got thin, and became a dreadful sight. And now I'm always in a sweat, and cough till I think I'm going to bring my heart up. And I can no longer spit. And I haven't the strength to stand, you see. I can't eat.'

"A stifling sensation made her pause, and she became livid…. She was unable to speak any further, for just then an attack of coughing shook her and threw her back upon the seat. She was suffocating, and the red flush on her cheekbones turned blue."[34]

Inevitably, there would be no long-term improvement in his health. From 1847 to 1850 he was well enough to do some teaching again, though his voice was scarcely audible because of his weak chest. In 1850, Louis asked Dufau to allow him to retire, but his pension being too small to live on, the director agreed to let him stay on in exchange for giving piano lessons from time to time.[35]

BRAILLE'S LAST LETTER HOME

Louis's last known letter to his mother was written in the fateful year of 1848. That February, rioting in Paris forced King Louis-Philippe to abdicate in favor of his grandson and seek refuge in England. There followed bloody rioting in the streets of Paris through July of 1848, a short-lived constitutional experiment in which Louis Napoleon (the supposed grandnephew of the first Bonaparte) served as president only to end as emperor after a plebiscite. Although his eighteen-year reign had given France stability and prosperity, this was not enough after the glory of Napoleon's Empire (the spilled blood of two decades of European warfare had been forgotten). "France is bored," wrote the foreign minister Lamartine — the same man to whom the Institution owed its new

building. Once again, the revolution had come full circle, from emperor back to emperor.

Throughout the uproar in the streets of Paris, Louis's illness kept him in his room at the Institution. Ever the country boy, he dwells in the following letter on the grape harvest, and summoned up the courage to face another winter — the hard season that invariably had a bad effect on his delicate health.

Paris, 15 November 1848

My dear mother,
Since I left you six weeks ago, I have had no news from you despite the passage of time, so I implore you to write to tell me if you are in good health and to chat about our relatives and the people you talk to about me from time to time.

I have noticed with pleasure that the weather has been as good as it can be during the grape harvest, but today the sun is very weak. The bad season is beginning and we must stay indoors. As for me, I do not go out, and while snow fell upon the heads of Parisians going to the feast of the [new] constitution, I was content to listen to the cannon shots from my little, well-heated room.

Very well, let us continue to be courageous as winter passes, and write to give me news of yourself, my brothers [Louis had only one; perhaps he called his

brothers-in-law "brother"] and my sisters, and our friends. I hope to come to see you at the end of the winter. Until that happy time, be assured once again of your son's affection.

L. Braille

FINAL DAYS

It is not known whether Louis managed to visit his mother in the spring of 1849. If he did, it would have been one of only a few more opportunities for him to be in Coupvray with family and friends. Three years later, Louis succumbed to the disease that had been gnawing at him for more than 25 years.

A. *Peru stamp: Louis Braille, in profile, looks almost Dickensian on this stamp marking the 150th anniversary of the braille system.* B. *DDR (East Germany) issued this commemorative stamp in 1975: World Braille Year. Louis's sunken cheeks and clenched jaw hint at his illness.* C. *This Luxembourg stamp reproduces the miniature on ivory created by Lucienne Filippi in 1966. The palm leaves on the lapels symbolize learning.* D. *Guyana stamp issued by the only country in South America whose official language is English. This stamp shows Louis Braille in his teacher's uniform and captures his youthful appearance better than most images.* E. *This Argentina stamp uses the image of Louis Braille taken from his death mask.*

GLOBAL BRAILLE

The tenacity of the students at INJA was a preview of what would later drive the dissemination of the braille code throughout the world. Blind people would insist (often in the face of opposition from well-meaning sighted people) that braille was much more practical than other reading and writing methods. This can be gauged from the following account of a French boy confidently using braille, as reported by Sir Francis Head in the *Cyclopedia of Useful Arts* in 1854.[1] The account appeared in England soon after France had accepted braille as the official means of teaching blind children.

"Not only are M. Braille's embossed symbols evidently better adapted to the touch than the letters and figures which have been so cleverly invented for the eyesight, but to the blind they possess an additional superiority of inestimable value, namely, that they, the blind, can not only read this type, but with the greatest possible ease make it, and as I witnessed this very interesting operation, I will endeavour briefly to describe it.

"A blind boy was required to write down before me, from the dictation of his blind professor, a long sentence. With a common awl, not only kept in line, but within narrow limits, by a brass groove which the writer had the power to lower at the termination of each line, the little fellow very rapidly poked holes [embossed dots] tallying with the letters he wished to represent. There was no twisting of his head sideways, no contortion of the face, no lifting up of his right heel, no screwing up of his mouth, no turning his tongue from beneath the nose towards one ear, and then towards the other, in sympathy with the tails of crooked letters, which in great pain and difficulty, in ordinary writing, the schoolboy may be seen successively endeavouring to transcribe.

"On the contrary, as the little fellow punched his holes, he sat as upright as a cobbler hammering at the sole of a shoe. On the completion of the last letter he threw down his awl, and then like a young author proudly correcting his press, with his forefinger instead of his eyes... he touched in succession every letter, and all proving to be correct, he stretched out his little hand and delivered to me his paper. To test the practical utility of the operation, a blind boy was sent for from another room. The embossed paper (for what was a hole on one side was, of course, a little mountain on the other) was put into his hands, and exactly as fast as his finger could pass over the protuberances made by his comrade, he read aloud the awled [sic] sentence that I had heard dictated. I may observe that besides letters and figures, notes of music are also done by the awl."[2]

THE CODE SPREADS

Although sighted people remained puzzled by the inscrutable pages of dots that bore no obvious relation to print, blind people took to braille wherever it was made available to them. The code had spread outside France as early as 1837, when it was adopted in Belgium for "special teaching" (it did not replace embossed print).[3] In 1852, writing in raised dots was accepted at the Asylum for

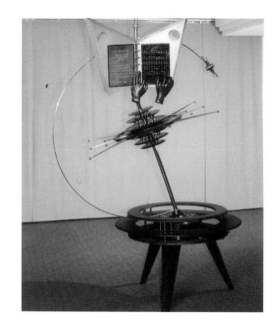

the Blind in Lausanne, Switzerland, the first institution outside France to do so.[4]

In the United States, the Missouri School for the Blind in, appropriately enough, St. Louis, Missouri, was the first institution to use braille — in 1854.[5] The students quickly learned and accepted it, not only because it was easy to read and write but also because their teachers could not understand it. Students could now send each other little notes — even love letters — and no busybody teacher could read them. The teachers, mainly sighted young women, understandably felt threatened by this new system. If blind people could readily understand braille, they could also teach it, thus jeopardizing the sighted teachers' jobs.

Empirical evidence for braille's superiority over embossed print was rarely collected, but such data could be found. In the United States, an analysis of the reports made by seven schools for the blind to their respective state legislatures (whose appropriations paid the bills) showed that of 664 students where Boston Line Type (a prevalent embossed print) was used, one-third learned to read fluently, one-third by a process of spelling, that is, reading letter by letter, and one-third failed. At the Missouri Institution, where "the French dotted character" (braille) was used, two-thirds learned to read fluently, one-third by spelling, while none failed. These statistics were reported by a blind physician, T.R. Armitage, in his book *The Education and Employment of the Blind. What It Has Been, Is, and Ought to Be.* He concluded that "those who learn to read by this system also acquire an admirable method of writing."[6]

UNIVERSAL SYSTEM OF READING AND WRITING

In 1873, a pioneering meeting took place, The Vienna Congress of Teachers of the Blind. These teachers, mainly from Europe but also from other continents, devoted much time to discussing the adoption of a generally acceptable reading and writing system. The contest was

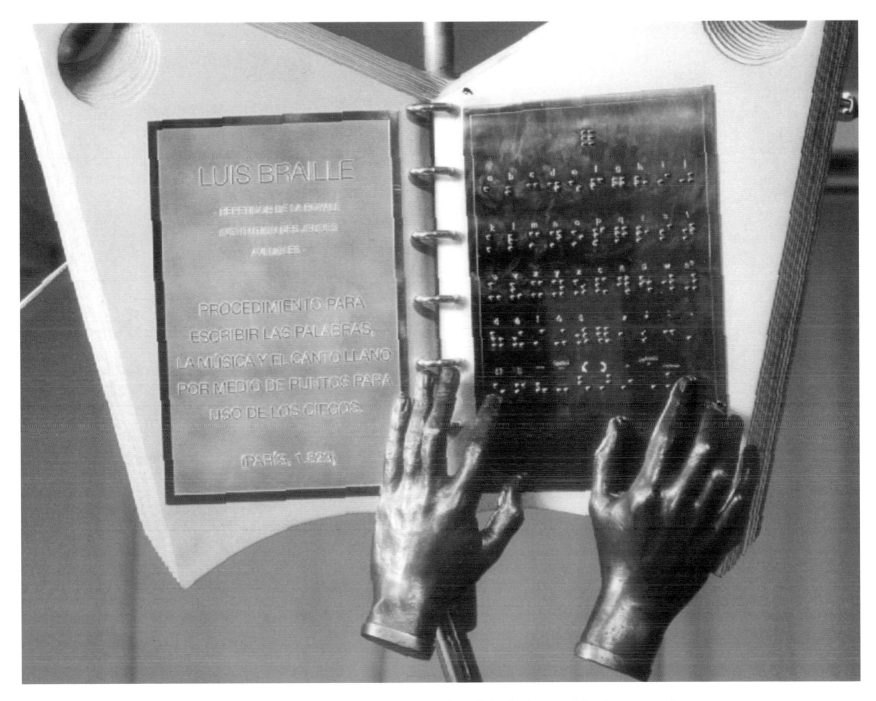

Above and facing page: Created by the blind artist César Delgado, this powerful sculpture graces the Museum for the Blind at the Spanish National Organization of the Blind (ONCE) in Madrid.

between braille and New York Point (a system of embossed dots rather like a braille cell turned on its side), but the only decision made was to elect a standing committee to study the problem. There seemed, however, to be much support for Point because it saved space. It was for this reason that even Louis Braille's student, Victor Ballu, favored Point, though he claimed to have invented a shorthand system based on braille that saved even more space than Point. At this date, Germany seemed to favor braille, while Brazil was actively using both literary and music braille.[7]

In continental Europe, a persistent difficulty was that different countries wanted to amend braille's original code so that the most frequently used letters in their own language were assigned to braille cells with the least number of dots.[8] A consequence was that if a blind person who knew French braille wanted to learn German, he or she had to learn a new alphabet as well as a new language. This immense difficulty was resolved in 1878 at an international meeting in Paris: the Congrès Universel pour l'amélioration du sort des aveugles et sourds-muets[9] attended by delegates from Germany, Great Britain, Austro-Hungary, Belgium, Denmark, France, Holland, Sweden, and Switzerland. A "strong" majority voted in favor of the general use of the unmodified braille code.[10] It is also significant

Students reading braille in Beijing, China.

that following this congress, the custom took hold of using the very word "braille" to refer to the code that the teenage Louis Braille had invented.[11]

In 1870, under the energetic prodding of T.R. Armitage (who actually spoke in favor of Point at the 1873 Vienna Congress!), Great Britain adopted the use of unmodified (French) braille for writing, but for embossed books decided to use Moon Type, a simplified form of embossed print letters.[12] Even so, by 1883, most British schools for the blind used braille.[13]

LAGGARD UNITED STATES

In the United States, the braille code's journey to full acceptance was long and painful. Braille had to compete with four

other widely used codes: (1) Boston Line Type, favored by the influential Samuel Gridley Howe; (2) Moon Type; (3) American braille (the French code modified); and (4) New York Point, the most successful embossed-dot competitor, devised in 1868 by William B. Wait, superintendent of the New York School for the Blind.[14]

The tactile Tower of Babel severely curtailed the access of blind people to reading materials, and it represented a distressing waste of resources on the production of different versions of the same book or document. In 1905, the absurd situation was summed up by Charles W. Holmes, president of the Alumni Association of the Perkins Institution for the Blind: "We have at present five distinct codes of embossed print, and virtual sub-divisions of some of them — since some books are printed with, and some without contractions.[15] In order to avail himself of the full range of literature… the blind reader must learn, and keep well up in, all these codes. How would our seeing friends stand for such a state of affairs in type?"[16] With the well-intended goal of making reading material available to blind children, the federal government subsidized the production of New York Point from 1879. (Not until 1894 was part of the subsidy used to produce braille texts.) Another barrier to the spread of braille was the tax imposed on braille books imported from the United Kingdom.[17]

Devotion to Louis Braille at the Red Cross School for the Blind, Berhampur, India.

UNIFORM TYPE COMMITTEE

A "Uniform Type Committee" was set up to make sense of this situation, which eventually boiled down to collecting empirical data to determine which of the three competing embossed types would become the standard. In Sir Clutha Mackenzie's words, "It was as if one-third of Americans spelled WASHINGTON in the ordinary way, one-third spelled it PXFTOQWSAQ, and the remainder ⋊ ⊢ ∫ ∽ ⋌ ⋋ ⊢ ⋝ ⋏ ⋊."[18]

The Uniform Type Committee conducted tests in which blind people read documents embossed in different systems in an attempt to obtain objective measures of the efficiency of each. William B. Wait conducted a spirited defense of his own New York Point. He seemed to think that acceptance of British braille would be tantamount to betraying the "Spirit of '76" and America's returning to membership in the British Empire. He accused the Uniform Type Committee of conducting a "diabolical project," engaging in "an audacious and shameful action" and demanding a "treacherous sacrifice."[19] Such overheated language was not unheard of in what became "The War of the Dots."[20] Expressing the frustrations of many, one blind person at a national convention of

the blind offered a tempting solution: "If anyone invents a new system of printing for the blind, shoot him on the spot."[21]

The voices of reason eventually prevailed, but not until 1932 was a uniform braille code accepted by the English-speaking world. It took almost twenty years longer — until 1951 — for the world's Spanish speakers to agree; Brazil and Portugal came to terms the following year.[22] Today, braille is used today in almost every country in the world, adapted to almost every known language from Albanian to Zulu.

But the battle over a "unified braille code" continues. While the first "War of the Dots" was over the structure of the braille cell and various characters, the current controversy is primarily based on whether or not there is a need to change braille at all, the elimination of some contractions, the use of print font indicators, and significant changes to the braille math code.

In 1991, the Braille Authority of North America and then later the International Council on English Braille embarked on an initiative to introduce and adopt a Unified English Braille Code for braille readers throughout the English-speaking world. Laudable as the goal is for improving on the code, braille readers are asking the question, "Will

Left: Frank H. Hall invented this typewriter-like machine for writing braille in 1892. It "delighted" those attending the convention of the American Association of Instructors of the Blind that year, where Hall's daughter wrote 100 words a minute on the machine. Below: A line of refreshable braille.

standardizing the code create more problems, or will the benefits outweigh the perceived liabilities?" These questions reflect the inquiries voiced by leaders in the blindness field over 100 years ago. Perhaps the answer is that now with modern braille transcription technologies, braille can be what it needs to be for all of its readers. But ultimately, braille belongs to its readers, and their voices must be heard and abided by in the crusade for unification.[23]

TECHNICAL DEVELOPMENTS

The diffusion of braille was accelerated in the late-19th and early-20th century by two technical improvements: the braillewriter and interpoint braille. The first successful machine to write braille was the Hall braillewriter, invented in 1892 and using the same principle as a typewriter, but with only six keys (one for each braille dot) and a space bar. Prototypes enabled an operator to braille 85 words per minute;[24] higher speeds were later achieved. Several other devices for writing braille have appeared over the years, but the most widely used now is the Perkins Brailler, first manufactured in 1951. The ability to interpoint braille doubled the amount of braille on a page by allowing dots to be embossed on both sides.[25]

The advent of computer technology has greatly improved the ability to produce and write braille. It is now possible to scan a print document into a computer, translate it from print into braille using special software, and emboss it on paper with a braille printer. Even more remarkable is an invention called "refreshable braille," wherein small pins move up and down in an electronic device to form various dot configurations. Once the reader has passed his or her fingers over the line, he or she presses a bar, and another new line appears. Such braille displays allow a blind person to read words displayed on a computer screen, including email, compose and edit documents, translate print documents "on the fly," download books online, and so on.

NON-EUROPEAN LANGUAGES

As a code, braille can stand for virtually anything, including any language (alphabetic or not), just as it can be used for music, mathematics, and computer notation. All that is required is a key to the code. The first adaptations of braille to non-European languages date from the 1870s and were mainly the work of missionaries from Europe and America. "Working in their distant outposts, they took pity on helpless blind children and gathering them into the missionary compounds, discovered... that they had founded pioneer schools for the blind."[26] The missionaries managed, with various degrees of success, to adapt the 63 braille signs to languages with long alphabets, thousands of ideographs, and, in Chinese languages, up to six tones. India's multitude of dialects presented such difficulties that, in 1949, India requested a meeting of UNESCO[27] to study the problem at an international level. (Under UNESCO sponsorship, uniformity in mathematical and scientific notation had been achieved at a 1929 congress in Vienna.)

International cooperation is still necessary today, since most groups understandably do not like to abandon methods that have proven workable for them, perhaps over many years. Standardization has also been stimulated by the widespread use of computers to produce and read braille. The stamps and other illustrations in this chapter vividly demonstrate the entire world's gratitude to Louis Braille for his brilliant and simple code that so efficiently signals its message to the fingertips.

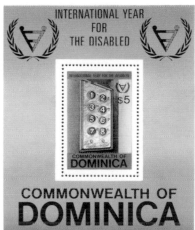

A. *This Mali stamp shows a more rugged Louis Braille. The larger dots in the background spell bra/ille.* **B.** *In this 1981 Panama stamp, Louis is described as the "creator of a reading and writing system for the blind."* **C.** *This stamp from Uruguay, issued in 1976, heralded 150 years of braille.* **D.** *The tiny Caribbean island of Dominica shows elevator controls marked in large print and braille.* **E.** *In 1959, Louis Braille was celebrated behind the Iron Curtain, where Cyrillic characters are used, as this stamp from the former Soviet Union shows. Here Louis assumes the appearance of a commissar.*

Epilogue

One of the most memorable events of my life was my visit to the village of Coupvray in France — the birthplace of Louis Braille. That day in June 1998, we delegates of the "Second International Conference on the Blind in History" entered the old church. Around the altar, I touched the serene carvings that spoke of answered prayers, reassurances. Then, Elizabeth, my companion, placed my hands on the stone font where Louis Braille, just four days old, had been baptized; and I wondered what life would be like without braille.

I was seven years old when my mother and teachers noticed I had an eye condition. Despite medical treatment, my eyesight deteriorated, and I was finally introduced to braille reading. I attended a Chicago public school that maintained a special department for visually impaired students. Admittedly, I shunned reading braille as much as I could. I was satisfied having my mother read books to me, and I memorized facts readily. Leisure time was spent listening to the radio or chatting with friends over the phone. How thrilled we blind students were with the first model of a recorded medium for reading — the talking book — that was brought to the school. Now we could read more books faster!

But, more and more, I was aware of a hearing loss. My mother had to read louder; I had to move closer and closer to the radio. I enjoyed talking books for less than a year. Profoundly deaf, I had to rely on my tactual sense for communicating and reading. For me, a teenage girl with exciting daydreams, the future looked hollow, just a hole out there in front of me.

Then the director of the Braille Department at school sent a note to my mother, saying, "Send Geraldine back to school. We want her to graduate with her classmates. We will transcribe all her textbooks and assignments into braille."

Rapidly, braille filled the empty hollow with possibilities. I turned to braille for learning, for employment (eventually working as an instructor at the Hadley School), and for entertainment. Although my family and close friends mastered special communication methods for those who are deaf, I still needed a universal method, a way to communicate with the public. One of the earliest universal methods was the alphabet card. This is a pocket-sized card with both the print and braille alphabet on it. Sighted persons can read the print letters and place my finger on the corresponding braille letters to spell words. For many deafblind people, social life was confined to braille-land. Braille-land is still a very active society of pen pals, round-robin clubs, and magazine forums. Our most welcome visitor is the mail carrier, bringing braille letters, library books, and magazines — these are our favorite things!

Around 1950, the American Foundation for the Blind developed the "Tellatouch" machine, a small portable typewriter with the keyboard on one side and a single refreshable braille cell on the other. Conversations can be carried on fluently by typing on the keyboard, while the deafblind conversant reads the letters rising from the braille cell. With the Tellatouch, I can talk with my neighbors, handle business transactions, and communicate with airline attendants. Computer technology has opened new doors: I now join my hearing and sighted friends by sending and receiving email messages and chatting over the phone — all because we have electronic devices with braille displays.

And so, with my hands on the stone basin where little Louis was baptized, I whispered, "Thank you."

— **Geraldine Lawhorn**

Directions to La Maison Natale de Louis Braille

If you wish to participate in this great effort to honor the memory of Louis Braille and make his birthplace more widely known, you can send your donations to: The Chairman of the Louis Braille Committee, 58, avenue Bosquet, 75007 Paris, France.

Travel Directions from Paris
The museum is located on the outskirts of Paris, near EuroDisney, and is easily accessible by road or train.

By automobile:
Take Autoroute A4 to exit 14, Disney/Paris/Coupvray.

By train from Paris:
Take the *Meaux* line from *Gare de l'Est*. Get off at *Esbly,* and then take a taxi to Coupvray.

By RER:
Take the "A" line to *Marne-la-Vallée/Disney,* about an hour's ride. Then take a taxi to Coupvray (about 10 minutes).

Eurostar trains from London:
Fast Eurostar trains run to Disney from London (Waterloo). Get out at *Marne-la-Vallée/Disney* and take a taxi to Coupvray (10 minutes).

Entrance fees:
Adults: €4.00 (children are free)
Groups: €3.00 per person
Students: €1.00

Hours:
Summer schedule (April 1st to September 30th)
Open daily, except Monday, 10 a.m. to noon and 2 p.m. to 6 p.m.
Winter schedule (October 1st to March 31st)
Open daily, except Monday (Friday by appointment) from 2 p.m. to 5 p.m.

To arrange for group tours and all other information, contact:
Maison Natale de Louis Braille
13, rue Braille
77700 Coupvray, France
Tel/fax: +33 (0) 1 60 04 82 80
Email: musee.braille@wanadoo.fr

Illustration Sources and Credits

LETTERS

Letters from *Louis Braille 1809-1852 Correspondence* (1999) courtesy of l'Institut National des Jeunes Aveugles (INJA Archives), pages 54, 66, 71, 87, 88, 89, 103.

Letter to Barbier courtesy of Musée Valentin Haüy, Paris, France, page 65.

ENGRAVINGS & LITHOGRAPHS

The Blind Girl of the Bridge (Pont Neuf), engraving by I. Pierre Simon after a painting by Jean Frédéric Schall (French painter, 1752-1825), page iv; *The Blind Man and the Tilbury*, lithograph by Miss Hubert after either Adolphe Eugène Gabriel Roehn (French painter, 1780-1867) or Alphonse Roehn (French painter, 1799-1864), page ix; Louis Braille, miniature on ivory by Lucienne Filippi, page xii; *The End of a Sad Day*, 1838 lithograph by M. Alophe (pseudonym for Adolphe Menut, French painter and photographer, 19th century), page 22; two country beggars (no title), engraving by Pierre Alexandre Wille (French painter and printmaker, 1748-1837), page 23; Nicholas Saunderson, engraving by F. Hinton after a graphic by J. Vanderbank, page 32; *Blind Beggars Scuffling*, engraving, Jacques Bellange (French painter, etcher, and draftsman, ca. 1575-1616), page 42; *The Blind Boy's Dog*, engraving by Dibart after a painting by Wafflard (French, first half of 19th century), page 47; Samuel Gridley Howe, first director Perkins School for the Blind, painting by Jane Stuart (1812-1888), page 52; The Quinze Vingts Neighborhood, Bouchoy (French, 1840-1850), page 70.

PHOTOGRAPHS AND ILLUSTRATIONS

All images courtesy of La Maison Natale de Louis Braille, Coupvray, France, except: l'Institut National des Jeunes Aveugles (INJA), Paris, France, pages 1, 2, 3, 28, 34, 44, 83, 100; Musée Valentin Haüy, Paris, France, pages 30, 31, 34, 37, 38, 53, 86 (those photographed by Christian Moutarde) pages 63, 65, 80, 92, 93, 96; Bibliothèque Valentin Haüy, Paris, France, page 35; Keller stamp, page 11, and Lincoln stamp, page 13, from Stamps of India Collectors Companion; Darwin stamp reproduced by kind permission of Royal Mail Group plc., page 13; Perkins School for the Blind, Watertown, MA, pages iv, ix, 22, 23, 33, 42, 47, 52; Smithsonian Institution Libraries, Washington, DC, page 32; American Foundation for the Blind, Helen Keller Archives, New York, NY, page 11; Leaning Tower of Pisa photographed by Abelardo Morell, Brookline, MA, page 33 (from *A Picture-Book for the Blind*); Encyclopédie, page 14; engravings from l'oeuvre des ateliers d'aveugles, a Paris (private collection of the author), pages 46, 48, 62; engravings from *An Essay on the Instruction and Amusements of the Blind*, S. Guillié, 1817 (private collection of the author), photographed by Len Morris Photography, New York, NY, pages 50-51, 55; Le quartier des quinze vingt [sic] (private collection of the author), page 70; ©Photothèque des Musées de la Ville de Paris, caricature parisienne Café des Aveugles (anonymous), page 91; Brown University Library, Providence, RI, page 99; reproduced by permission of the artist, César Delgado, Madrid, Spain, pages 108-109; reproduced by permission of Miss Peng, Beijing School for the Blind, Beijing, China, page 110; Bhima Bhoi School for the Blind, Orissa, India, page 111; refreshable braille photographed by Rebecca Sherwood, page 112.

Endnotes

PROLOGUE

[1] Hippolyte Coltat, *Inauguration du buste de Louis Braille*, 1853, p. 25.

[2] Ibid., p. 25.

[3] A-R. Pignier, *Notices biographiques sur trois professeurs*, 1859, pp. 23-27.

[4] Coltat 1853, p. 24.

[5] Ibid., p. 25.

[6] Ibid., p. 24.

[7] Pignier 1859, p. 9.

[8] This society ran workshops where blind people could learn a skill that would help them become self-supporting, or continue to ply the trade they had mastered before becoming blind.

[9] Jean Roblin, *Les doigts qui lisent*, 1951, p. 112.

[10] Jouffroy's marble bust was unveiled at the Institution on May 25, 1853.

[11] Ibid., p. 15 and p. 22.

[12] Coltat 1853, p. 22.

[13] *The New York Times*, Sunday, June 22, 1952. "Helen Keller Pays Tribute to Braille." It is unlikely that Helen Keller was capable of speaking French — or any language — very clearly. Though several skilled teachers tried to enable her to speak, they met with little success. Helen could manage a few more or less intelligible words, but throughout her life regarded her inability to speak clearly as her most serious handicap.

[14] *The New York Times*, Monday, June 23, 1952. "A Century of Braille."

HOME

[1] Roblin 1951, p.24.

[2] To understand precisely what Simon-René's trade was, it is useful to distinguish between the *bourrelier* and the *sellier* (saddler). The latter made equipment for those who *rode* horses, while the former made equipment for those who used the horse as a source of power.

[3] Roblin 1951, p. 20.

[4] In this account of the Braille family, I have drawn heavily on J. Roblin's *Les doigts qui lisent*, Paris, 1951.

[5] Constantius Cephalis wrote a note stating: "the right eye when diseased often gives its suffering to the left." Quoted in Duke Elder S. and Perkins E.S. in *System of Ophthalmology*, Vol. IX, "Diseases of the uveal tract."

[6] In 1830, William Mackenzie (1791-1868) noted in the first edition of *A Practical Treatise on the Diseases of the Eye* that inflammation of the second eye was dependent on the first, and he applied the term "sympathetic ophthalmia" to it. Cited in Medow, Norman, "Sympathetic ophthalmia not fully understood 100 years later..." *Ophthalmology Times*, June 15, 2003.

[7] I am indebted to Dr. Marvin Sears, professor emeritus of ophthalmology at Yale, for drawing my attention to this current understanding of sympathetic ophthalmia.

[8] Coltat 1853, p. 14.

[9] Roblin 1951, p. 29, plus details from Margaret Calvarin, the curator at the museum.

[10] In 1952, the Braille family home was sold to the association "Les Amis de Louis Braille" (The Friends of Louis Braille) and converted into a museum. In 1994, the Louis Braille Committee, under the auspices of the World Blind Union, applied to the French Directorate of Museums to have the museum reclassified as a national museum. The Directorate recommended instead that the museum be reclassified as a historic site, and the name was officially changed from Le Musée Louis Braille to La Maison Natale de Louis Braille (from *Braille Into the Next Millennium*, p. 100).

[11] The World Blind Union represents over 50 million blind and visually impaired people around the world. Several WBU officers were instrumental in preserving the Louis Braille home and museum, including Dr. Kenneth Jernigan of the United States,

Sir Duncan Watson of the United Kingdom, Dr. Euclid Herie of
Canada, Enrique Elissalde representing Latin America, David
Blyth of Australia, and Pedro Zurita of Spain.

12 Euclid J. Herie is former president of both the Canadian National
Institute for the Blind (1983-2001) and the World Blind Union
(1996-2000).

13 Dr. Kenneth Jernigan (1926-1998), served many years as
president, then president emeritus, of the National Federation of
the Blind in Baltimore, Maryland, where he led numerous organi-
zational initiatives to promote braille. He went to Coupvray in
1995, as part of a successful fund-raising drive to help repair and
restore Louis Braille's home.

14 The full text of Herie's tour can be found in "La Maison Natale de
Louis Braille," *Braille Into the Next Millennium*, 2000. Library of
Congress, Washington DC, pp. 73-105.

COUPVRAY

1 Note how he does not dwell at all on his poor health: this was in
late 1847, and by then he knew that he was doomed.

2 Frances Koestler, *The Unseen Minority*, New York, McKay, 1976, p. 3.
Paperback edition, American Foundation for the Blind, 2004.

3 *Etat des aveugles dans la commune de Coupvray* (The condition of blind
people in Coupvray), 1831. Cited in Roblin 1951, p. 27.

4 Samuel Gridley Howe in *Address of the Trustees of the New-England
Institution for the Education of the Blind* (1833), p. 4.

5 Roblin 1951, p. 55.

6 Ibid., p. 32, fn. 19.

7 The poor harvest in 1816, "the year without a summer," was the result
of a colossal eruption of Mount Tambora in the Pacific the year
before. See "Blast from the Past," *Smithsonian*, July 2002, pp. 53-57.

8 Many devout people in those days thought that to inject human
beings with a disease that they might never catch was to tempt
Providence. See *The Memoirs of Chancellor Pasquier 1767-1815*, p. 2.

9 Roblin 1951, p. 32.

10 Ibid., p. 33.

11 Ibid., p. 37.

12 Ibid., p. 38.

13 Ibid., pp. 39-40.

14 Ibid., p. 39. By a remarkable coincidence, M. d'Orvilliers had
purchased his Coupvray chateau in 1791 from Louis-Rene-
Edouard de Rohan, who was superior general of the Quinze-
Vingts, a fraternal residential charity for blind people in Paris.

15 Virginia was the name of his sister-in-law.

16 Marie-Céline's family.

17 A popular card game, similar to whist, invented in Boston,
Massachusetts, and introduced to Paris by Benjamin Franklin.

VALENTIN HAÜY

1 Although it is often written that Louis was the youngest student at
the school, the Registre des Entrées shows that he was not.

2 Henri 1952, p. 12. Among the prisoners was Abbé René-Just
Haüy, Valentin's brother. His crime was his refusal to swear an
oath of loyalty to the new regime. He was unperturbed.
Accustomed to spartan surroundings and relaxed to be among
friends, he asked his guardians merely to bring him his precious
collection of minerals and his cabinet of drawers, which had been
overturned during his arrest, so that he could put the mineral collection back in order. He might well have lost his life if powerful
friends had not interceded with officers of the revolution. *The
Mineralogical Record*, November 1, 1994.

3 From Lamartine's report, cited by Roblin 1951, p. 99.

4 Sébastien Guillié, *Rapport*, 1818, p. 28.

5 At the New-England Institution for the Blind in Boston, "strict
cleanliness was required, and every pupil had an opportunity of
having a warm bath as often as desirable." (*Annual Report*, 1835, p. 13.)

6 The date on which Haüy witnessed this spectacle is not certain. Weygand 2003, p. 111, gives 1771 as the most likely date.

7 For a brief history of the Quinze-Vingts, in both English and French, see Z. Weygand, "The Quinze-Vingts from their Founding until the Beginning of the Nineteenth Century"/ "Les Quinze-Vingts, depuis leur fondation jusqu'au début du XIXe siècle" in: *Second International Conference on the Blind in History and the History of the Blind*, 1998, pp. 158-183.

8 Zina Weygand, *Vivre sans voir*, 2003, pp. 111-112.

9 Valentin Haüy, *Essai sur l'éducation des aveugles*, p. 119. He used different descriptions of his experience over the years. See Weygand 2003, p. 113.

10 Abbé René-Just Haüy in fact dedicated his life to science and was founder of the science of mineralogy.

11 Peter Gay, *The Enlightenment v.1*, 1966, p. 3.

12 For a highly readable account of the British, French, and American enlightenments, see Gertrude Himmelfarb, *The Roads to Modernity*, Knopf 2004. Heretical opinions can be found in Christopher O. Blum (ed.), *Critics of the Enlightenment*, ISI Books, 2004.

13 Arthur M. Wilson, *Diderot*, 1972, p. 100.

14 He was not incarcerated in a cell but was detained in a tower at Vincennes, an imposing medieval fortress and former royal residence six miles east of Paris, from July through November. For such a social man, the solitary confinement was very distressing, and the visitors he was eventually allowed described Diderot as "greatly affected" by imprisonment.

15 Wilson 1972, p. 100.

16 This information is taken from a life of Saunderson affixed to: Saunderson, Nicholas, *The Elements of Algebra*, 1740, published after his death, and from Wilson, J. 1821, *Biography of the Blind*, pp. 205-216.

17 Nicholas Saunderson, *Elements of Algebra*, 1740, Vol. I, p. iii.

18 W. Artman and L.V. Hall, *Beauties of the Blind*, pp. 221-224.

19 Saunderson 1740, Vol. I, p. vii.

20 Denis Diderot, *Letter*, translated 1773, p. 45.

21 Ibid., p. 14.

22 *Journal de Paris*, Sept 30, 1784. Cited in Weygand 2003, p. 116.

23 Quoted in Weygand, "Maria Theresia von Paradis," *Voir barré*, December 2001, p. 94.

24 Ibid., p. 95. Dr. Weygand suggests that these arrangements were made, at least in part, to raise funds to help meet her travel expenses.

25 Kempelen was famous across Europe as inventor of the "Turk," a chess-playing automaton that created the illusion that it was playing chess; it was, in fact, operated by a man concealed inside it.

26 Haüy 1786, p. 61.

27 Ibid.

28 Pamela Lorimer, *Reading by Touch*, 2000, p. 18.

29 J.R. Briscoe (ed.), *Historical Anthology of Music by Women*, 1987, pp. 94-100.

30 For examples of von Paradis's music see *Voir barré*, December 2001, p. 97.

31 Haüy 1786, pp. 120-121.

32 Founded in 1780 mainly under the leadership of Freemasons. This was the first charitable institution in France not to be concerned with the soul, and not to have a religious management.

33 This version of Haüy's meeting with Le Sueur is based on Weygand's research published in *Vivre sans voir*, p.115, and differs from the more widely reported and romantic version, such as that in Henri, 1952, where Haüy meets Le Sueur completely by chance outside a church.

34 Roblin 1951, p. 47.

35 Weygand 2003, p. 115.

36 Henri 1984, p. 51.

37 Weygand 2003, p. 121.

38 Ibid.

39 An English translation of this work by Thomas Blacklock, a blind Scottish poet, was published in 1793 by Alexander Chapman and Company. According to Michael Anagnos, this translation was "remarkable for its inaccuracies." An online version can be found at http://www.aph.org/museum/huaymain.html.

40 Guillié, *Rapport* 1818, p. 37. Rouillé de l' Etang (1731-1811) was a member of the Paris Hospital Council from 1810 until his death.

41 M. Galliod, *Notice historique sur l'Etablissement des Jeunes Aveugles*, 1828, p. 4.

42 Messieurs Desmarets, Demours, Vicq-d'Azir (personal physician to Marie-Antoinette) and M. le Duc de Rochefoucauld (a great philanthropist, member of the Philanthropic Society, and the Royal Societies of Medicine and of Agriculture).

43 Extrait des registres de l'Académie, pp. 10-11.

44 *Fiftieth Annual Report*, Perkins Institution and Massachusetts School for the Blind, September 30, 1881, p. 67. Written by Michael Anagnos, director, (son-in-law of Samuel Gridley Howe).

45 Haüy wisely arranged public demonstrations of his methods for the duel purpose of raising funds and to show that blind people could, in fact, be taught and become productive citizens. (Haüy 1786, pp. 9-14.)

46 Haüy and the children actually performed two concerts at Versailles — one for the king and his family and another before the king and his ministers. The second of the performances evidently impressed the Marquis d'Orvilliers, a nobleman from Coupvray. He remembered it 30 years later, and agreed to help Louis Braille attend the school in Paris. Weygand 2003, pp. 126, 139-140.

47 Simon Schama, *Citizens*, 1989, p. 189.

48 *Fiftieth Annual Report*, Perkins Institution, 1881, p. 68. Anagnos was writing long before Verdun, Passchendaele, Auschwitz, Hiroshima, and the Gulag.

49 Ibid.

50 Weygand 2003, p. 167.

51 Years later, when Abbé Sicard was arrested as an enemy of the Revolution, Haüy's involvement was suspected. Though Haüy denied it, rancor between the two men intensified. Two friends of Sicard, Guillié and Dufau, eventually became directors of the school for the blind and were hostile to anyone partial to Haüy, including another director, Alexandre-René Pignier, who became a mentor to Louis Braille. As an administrator (Trustee) of the school, Sicard's influence was far-reaching.

52 Weygand 2003, p. 164.

53 *Fiftieth Annual Report*, Perkins Institution, 1881, p. 69.

54 Weygand 2003, p. 167.

55 *Fiftieth Annual Report*, Perkins Institution, 1881, p. 69.

56 Guillié, *Rapport* 1818, p. 7.

57 Théophilanthropy effectively ended in 1801 when the First Consul returned all the churches that had practiced "natural religion" to the Catholic Church, and forbade public meetings of the Théophilanthropists.

58 Weygand 2003, p.201, endnote 78, examines evidence of Haüy's involvement with the Freemasons. The role of Freemasons in humanitarian activity is fascinating and worth further study. Masons were prominent in the Philanthropic Society, and founded the *Journal de Paris*.

59 Ibid., p. 191.

60 Henri 1984, p. 113.

61 Ibid.

62 Weygand 2003, p. 206.

63 Henri 1984, pp. 119-120.

64 Ibid., pp. 104-105.

65 Weygand 2003, p. 282.

66 Ibid., p. 297.

67 Bouret was among those who had stormed the Bastille on July 14, 1789.

68 Henri 1984, p. 123.

69 Weygand 2003, p. 291.

70 Chaptal did Trojan work in reforming, among other things, the hospitals of Paris and improving midwifery services. Valentin Haüy was a nuisance, but hardly the most important challenge facing the Interior Minister; his larger battles were with Napoleon. The only Haüy name to appear in Chaptal's memoirs, *Mes souvenirs*, was fellow-scientist, René-Just Haüy, Valentin's brother.

71 President Lincoln's immortal Gettysburg Address opens with this archaic manner of counting: "Fourscore and seven years ago our fathers...."

72 By the sixteenth century, the "uniform" of a beggar from the Q-V consisted of a gown and cloak made of greenish blue cloth, upon which was sewn a fleur de lys insignia, to distinguish them from other blind beggars. Weygand 1998, p. 164. [French and English.]

73 Ibid., p. 174.

74 Cardinal Louis de Rohan is said to have obtained a bribe of 300,000 livres. Vaughan, Ernest, *Notice historique sur les Quinze-Vingts*, 1909, p. 6. It was the chateau of this same Rohan family that was bought in 1791 by Louis Braille's benefactor the Marquis d'Orvilliers. See Chapter "Coupvray."

75 Dora B. Weiner, *The Citizen-Patient in Revolutionary and Imperial Paris*, 1993, p. 246.

76 At a July 1850 meeting of the Société de Patronage et de Secours, a charitable society of which Louis Braille was a member and present at the meeting, some criticized the policies of the Quinze-Vingts for establishing pensions for young blind people, and in so doing, depriving them of the incentive to work. *Annales de l'éducation des sourds-muets et des aveugles*, Vol. 7, 1850, pp. 30-61.

77 Weygand 2003, p. 288.

78 Guillié, *Rapport* 1820, p. 12.

79 Weygand 1998, pp. 158-182. [French and English.]

SCHOOL LIFE

1 Director, Perkins School for the Blind, Boston, Massachusetts, 1907-1931.

2 This site is now occupied by a post office building. On the occasion of the 150th anniversary of Louis Braille's death, a plaque was posted in front of the building: *Louis Braille 1809-1852. L'inventeur du braille a conçu son système universel à cet emplacement lorsque l'Institut des Jeunes Aveugles s'y trouvait de 1816 à 1843 — INJA 2002.* (Translation: The inventor of braille conceived his universal system on this site, where the Institute for Young Blind was located from 1816 to 1843.)

3 Guillié, *Rapport* 1818, p. 15.

4 There were also occasional supplements, including 10,000 francs from King Louis XVIII in 1816, 10,371 francs from the royal treasury in 1817, and 5,000 francs from the king in 1818.

5 Guillié, *Rapport* 1820, p. 16.

6 Ibid., p. 34. Guillié was familiar with Cadet-de-Vaux's experiments to provide a tasty "economic soup" for distribution to poor people in Paris. See also Weiner 1993, p. 25.

7 Guillié, *Rapport* 1820, p. 33.

8 Maurice de la Sizeranne, *Guadet et les aveugles, sa vie, ses doctrines, ses écrits*, 1885, describes Guillié as "intelligent, habile, mais un peu charlatan," p. 129.

9 The French expression used by Joseph Guadet, later director of the Institution, was that Guillié ran the school, "avec une grande habilité dans l'art difficile de faire valoir les choses" (... with great skill in the difficult art of making things look good). Quoted in Weygand 2003, p. 317.

10 Of the 43 children who were refused admittance, 14 were sent home to their families; 12 received external Quinze-Vingts pensions of 150 francs; 7 had eyesight and were expected to make a living like other sighted children; 5 were admitted to the Quinze-Vingts hospital; 3 went to the Salpetrière, a prison/workhouse where vagabonds were held; and 2 to Bicêtre hospice.

11 Guillié, *Rapport* 1818, p. 16.

12 Roblin 1951, p. 49. For comparison, at the Yorkshire School for the Blind in England, it was found that "when patience and kindness are properly employed, severity is unnecessary." *Second Report*, 1838, p. 2.

13 From a May 1821 report to the Interior Ministry quoted in Weygand 2003, p. 318.

14 Roblin 1951, p. 49.

15 Guillié, *Rapport* 1818, p. 21.

16 Guillié removed from the library any books "offensive to modesty and religion." Ibid., p. 38.

17 Quoted in Henri 1952, p. 29.

18 Guillié, *Rapport* 1818, p. 20.

19 At the Quinze-Vingts, music was taught only to a select few children.

20 Guillié, *Rapport* 1820, p. 18.

21 Ibid., p. 18.

22 *The North American Review*, XXXVII, 1833, p. 9.

23 Guillié, *Essai* 1819, p. 215.

24 Ibid., p. 241.

25 Louis Braille later knew the man who had enthusiastically enforced Napoleon's control of the press in 1810: He was M. Portalis, son of Duke Jean-Etienne-Marie Portalis, a lawyer and one of the architects of the Civil Code. Portalis fils lasted less than a year as the government's chief censor before he was dismissed by the Emperor for allowing the distribution of a pamphlet criticizing his candidate for archbishop of Paris. Portalis endured a humiliating "furious verbal flagellation by the emperor before his council of state that lasted over an hour" before losing his job. It is in the house of this same Portalis that Louis Braille attended meetings of the Société de Patronage et de Secours pour les Aveugles Travailleurs en France, of which Portalis was first president. By the time Louis Braille knew him, in 1850, Portalis was first president of the Court of Cassation, the nation's highest tribunal. See Woloch, *Napoleon and his Collaborators* 2001 p. 158.

26 Guillié, *Essai* 1817, pp. 124 125.

27 Guillié, *Essai* 1819, pp. 85-86.

28 Guillié, *Rapport* 1818, p. 24.

29 Z. Weygand, "De l'expérience de Cheselden (1728) aux expériences du docteur Guillié sur l'ophtalmie contagieuse (1819-1920)." In *Histoire des Sciences Médicales*, Vol XXXIV, No. 3, 2000, pp. 295-304.

30 Guillié, *An Essay on the Instruction and Amusements of the Blind*. [English translation reprinted in 1894.]

31 Samuel Gridley Howe [writing anonymously], "Education of the Blind," *North American Review*, XXXVII, 1833, p. 18.

32 *Address of the Trustees of the New-England Institution for the Education of the Blind to the Public*, Boston, 1833, p. 7.

33 The 1836 *Transactions of the Society of Arts for Scotland* shows no less than 16 alphabets under consideration for use by the blind. Not one was successful. Moon Type, invented by a blind Englishman in 1847, and based mainly on highly simplified shapes of print, was produced in Great Britain throughout the 20th century.

34 Henri 1952, p. 22.

35 Weygand 2003, p. 319.

36 Pignier 1859, p. 9.

37 Ibid., pp. 9-10.

38 In French, Braille is pronounced "bry."

39 Weygand 2003, p. 349, explains that this was for an essay.

40 L. Montigny, *Le Provincial à Paris*, p. 258. Cited in Weygand 2003, p. 335.

41 Roblin 1951, p. 66.

42 Charles Barbier, *Essai sur divers procédés d'expéditive française, contenant douze écritures différentes, avec une planche pour chaque procédé*, Paris 1815. Cited in Weygand 2003, pp. 327-328.

43 Quoted in Weygand 2003, p. 330.

44 Ibid.

45 Letter from Barbier to Pignier, April 24, 1821; cited in Weygand 2003, p. 330.

46 The difficulties for blind harpists stem from "the painful position of the body and the multiplicity of strings undistinguished from each other," Guillié explained. Guillié 1819, p. 204.

BRAILLE CODE

1 U.S. writer and physician, 1809-1894. Founder of the *Atlantic Monthly*.

2 Pignier had been the doctor at the large and influential St. Sulpice seminary.

3 In his 1818 *Rapport*, p. 34, fn 1, Guillié mentions the "'embonpoint de la plupart' of our students."

4 Cited in Weygand 2003, p. 324.

5 Jardin des Plantes, just a few blocks east of the Institute.

6 Howe 1833, *Address of the Trustees...*, p. 15.

7 Several forces worked against Haüy's success in Russia. For one thing, France was at war with Russia and Haüy faced strong anti-French prejudice. For another, it proved difficult to recruit either competent teachers or reliable students. Struggling without success to acquire pupils the first year, he was told, "We have no blind people in Russia." (Roblin 1984, p. 140.)

8 Alexis de Noailles, an administrator of the institution who supported Pignier's openness to Haüy, had been ambassador in St. Petersburg when Haüy was there. At Noailles's behest, the czar bestowed upon Haüy a modest honor: cross (fourth class) of the order of St. Vladimir. Henri 1984, p. 150.

9 Henri 1984, p. 187.

10 Henri 1984, p. 188 refers to accounts of Braille's meeting Haüy as *romans*, i.e., fiction.

11 Weygand 2003, p. 330.

12 Roblin 1951, p. 61.

13 According to Abbé C. Carton, *Le Muet et l'aveugle*, Vol II, p. 85, Barbier's goal was to give blind people books that they could print themselves because his method [did not] require complicated typesetting.

14 The authors of this report were two very distinguished scientists: De Lacépède was a naturalist, a former student of Buffon, and highly respected by Napoleon. Ampère's investigations into the nature of electricity made him immortal through the universally used unit of electrical current, the "amp." *Rapport de Messieurs de Lacépède et Ampère sur l'écriture imaginée pour les aveugles par Monsieur Charles Barbier*, December 1, 1823. Cited in Weygand 2003, p. 332.

15 Courtesy INJA. Transcription by Martine Galtier. Translation by C.M. Mellor.

16 One of the wooden slates (réglettes) used to write the Barbier code is on display in the AVH Museum.

17 Weygand 2003, p. 332.

18 Pignier 1859, p. 14. Pignier makes no mention of a meeting between the haughty military officer and the scrawny teenage boy that appears in some modern accounts.

19 Ibid., pp. 17-18.

20 Ibid., p. 18.

21 The calculation is as follows: 2 to the power of 6, minus one, equals 63.

22 Henri 1952, p. 68.

23 Pignier 1859, p. 16.

24 Ibid., pp. 16-17.

25 *Procédé pour écrire les paroles, la musique et le plain-chant au moyen de points, à l'usage des aveugles*, et disposé pour eux par L. Braille, répétiteur à l'institution royale des jeunes aveugles, Paris. (*Procedure for writing words, music and plain-chant by means of dots, for use by the blind*, and prepared for them by L. Braille, repeater at the royal institution for young blind people, Paris.)

26 Quoted in Weygand 2003, p. 337.

27 Provided that he did not get entangled in a traffic jam — for which Paris was notorious even then.

28 Barbier seems to have developed a 3-dot code to simplify his system. Abbé C. Carton describes this in his *Le sourd-muet et l'aveugle*, 1827, Vol. II, p. 82.

29 This hand-written letter is preserved at INJA.

TEACHER

1 The address written by hand on this letter contains several mistakes that hint at the barely adequate level of literacy among those who could see: *Monsieur Monsieur [twice] pinier directeur delinstitution des jeune aveugle rue Saint Victor à Paris.*

2 Henri 1952, p. 30.

3 Roblin 1951, p. 71.

4 A politician and historian, Thiers (1797-1877) later became first president of the Third Republic (1871-73).

5 Henri 1952, p. 31.

6 Ibid.

7 Pignier 1859, p. 11.

8 Coltat 1853, p. 16.

9 Ibid., p. 21.

10 Coltat 1853, pp. 21-22. It should be noted that Coltat's remarks were made at the inauguration of the bust of Louis Braille at the Institution in 1853, and would therefore be of a flattering nature. Still, his account is the most informative known.

11 Roblin 1951, p. 70.

12 From an obituary at Perkins School in Boston, MA.

13 Coltat 1853, p. 23.

14 Pignier was a bachelor and had no children of his own. This refers to his students, whom he regarded as "his children."

15 Pignier 1859, p. 8.

16 The cause of Simon-René's death is unknown, but his symptoms, as described in this letter, are consistent with an enlarged prostate causing extremely painful retention of urine.

17 Monique died July 29, 1854, at the age of 85.

18 Louis-Simon is mistaken about the date, which was May 30.

19 Roblin 1951, p. 52.

20 Dr. Pignier's sister, with whom he lived, used to help both male and female repeaters to teach various trades. See Roblin 1951, p. 72, fn. 7.

21 "Carron 1832" is written outside the letter, in the same neat handwriting that appears inside, suggesting the scribe was one of his nephews, Louis-François or Louis-Théodore Carron.

22 By now Louis was hoarse and coughing chronically from consumption.

23 Pignier 1859, pp. 11-12.

24 This does not refer to James Frazer's famous *Golden Bough*, which was published in 1890.

MUSIC

1 English critic and stylist, proponent of "art for art's sake."

2 Henri 1952, p. 123.

3 Harvey Horatio Miller, professor of music emeritus, Brevard College, from *Braille Into the Next Millennium*, p. 129.

4 Henri 1952, p. 60, cites Edgar Guilbeau and claims that he probably obtained this information from some of Braille's contemporaries, whom he knew as a young man.

5 Better known as a social philosopher; his *Social Contract* (1762) strongly influenced the French Revolution. His novel *Emile* (1762) presented his theories of education.

6 Some of this information was gleaned from H. Miller, "The Braille Music Code," *Braille Into the Next Millennium*, pp. 137-139.

7 Those learning braille music are taught *never* to think of the notes in terms of the print letters also represented by the embossed dots. Richard Taesch and William McCann, *Who's Afraid of Braille Music???*, 2003, p. 9.

8 "Do" does not necessarily represent "C." In the "Moveable Do" system, "do" becomes the first scale step, regardless of which note the scale begins on.

9 A 32nd note uses the same symbol as a half note, and a 64th note uses the same symbol as a quarter note.

10 Roblin 1951, p. 66.

11 In high and low octaves, notes in print music are so difficult to read that they are usually printed for a lower (or higher) octave, with an instruction to play them an octave higher or lower.

12 Fred Neukomm, quoted in Henry Robyn, "Report to the Trustees, Principals and Teachers in Blind Asylums," St. Louis, MO, 1866, p. 5.

13 Adapted from Bettye Krolick, *How to Read Braille Music: An Introduction*, 1998, p. 2.

14 Efforts were made in the 20th century to unify the music braille code internationally. Bettye Krolick's *New International Manual of Braille Music Notation* (1966) is the most current compilation of the unified code, although the preface states that "... some traditional signs of one country or the other were not accepted in the voting."

15 Krolick's *How to Read Braille Music* (1998) is a lucid description of the braille music code. I would like to thank Bettye Krolick and Larry Smith for their advice on this section.

16 Richard Taesch, head of the Braille Music Division, Southern California Conservatory of Music, tells of a blind student who reads braille jazz chord progressions with her right hand while playing them with her left, up to tempo — this with music she had never read before, and in *live* performance. Another young blind violinist, after two days' practice with braille music, had to wait in rehearsal for the sighted children to catch up with her. I wish to thank Mr. Taesch for these examples and for his invaluable comments on this section.

17 George Shearing (with Alyn Shipton), *Lullaby of Birdland: The Autobiography of George Shearing*, 2004, p. 30.

18 Krolick 1998, p. 17.

19 His playing was described as "precise, brilliant, and free." Pignier 1859, p. 8.

20 The great cathedral of Saint-Etienne in Meaux has a centuries-long tradition of fine organ music. The instrument Louis Braille would have played was inaugurated in 1627, and was built by Valéran de Heman. This same organ was restored in 1980.

21 He was given free board and paid 300 francs as a teacher at the school.

22 It is tempting to think that this is the misspelled name of Palluy, Louis's very first teacher, who had been a canon at Meaux since 1826; he would have been 77 in 1832.

23 Charles Carton was director of the Institute for deaf-mutes and the blind in Bruges, Belgium.

24 Armitage 1871, pp. 27-30.

25 Braille made a little joke by signing his letter "Louis Jean Philippe." Louis-Philippe (1773-1850) was king of the French between 1830-1848. Louis Braille actually met Louis-Philippe on May 1, 1834, when the king opened the Exposition of Industry where Braille was demonstrating his reading and writing system. Roblin 1951, p. 78.

DOT-MATRIX PRINTING

1 A student of Louis Braille.

2 Braille's dictated letters were extremely difficult even to transcribe, let alone to translate.

3 L. Braille, *Nouveau procédé pour représenter par des points la forme même des lettres, les cartes de geographie, les figures de géométrie, les caractères de musique, etc., à l'usage des aveugles*, 1839, pp. 3-4. "New Procedure for representing by means of dots the precise shape of letters, geographical maps, geometrical shapes, musical notes, etc., for use by the blind."

4 Ibid., p. 5.

5 Ibid., p. 10.

6 Coltat 1853, p. 17. Louis's statement cleverly parodies Seneca's, *Plus sonat quam valet* — "more din than sense." Seneca, Epistles, XL, 5. Quoted in *The Essays of Michel de Montaigne*, translated by M.A. Screech, 1991, p. 192. Latin was taught at the Institution and Louis evidently was well versed in it.

7 Weygand, "Un clavier pour les aveugles," *Voir barré*, December 2001, p. 36.

8 C.J. Kudlick and Z. Weygand, *Reflections*, 2001. A superb biography of Thérèse-Adèle Husson, depicting the hard life of a poor blind couple in post-Revolutionary France.

9 Nine other novels by Husson were published, some posthumously, but the amount she received from publishers was scandalously little. See Kudlick & Weygand 2001.

10 Weygand, *Voir barré*, December 2001, p. 36.

11 Foucault in turn acknowledged that without Braille's "admirable" table of numbers, he would not have succeeded so well. The table was sold for one franc by the Institution. See Dufau 1850, p. 134, fn. 1.

12 Letter dated 17 May 1844, written by Foucault using a raphi-graphe.

13 The Great Exhibition of 1851 was the prototype of the world's fairs that in the 19th and 20th centuries celebrated industrial prowess and achievement. For Foucault to be invited to demonstrate his printing machine was a notable distinction.

14 It is not clear if this was identical to the raphigraphe. It might have been the two-keyboard printer, each with 30 keys, described by Dufau 1850, pp. 136-137. This seems to have been a precursor of the typewriter, since each key produced one print letter.

15 Prize medals were awarded to exhibitors who demonstrated "a certain standard of excellence in production or workmanship." See Asa Briggs, *Victorian Things*, 2003, p. 54.

16 Charles Tomlinson (ed.), *Cyclopedia of Useful Arts*, London, 1854, Vol. 2, p. 504.

17 The first working typewriter had been built in Italy in 1808 to help a blind countess, Carolina Fantoni da Fivizzono. Print type-writers were not produced on any scale until the 1870s.

18 I take this opportunity to thank Marc Dauw at Centrale Bibliotheek, Koninklijk M.P.I. Spermalie, Bruges, for his graciously receiving me and allowing me to hold this letter (inside its protec-tive covering) up to the light to make the tiny holes visible.

19 Ramon de la Sagra was a wealthy Spanish philanthropist, anarchist, traveler, and sometime director of the Botanical Gardens in Havana, Cuba.

20 After Etienne Denis Pasquier's election to the Academy, he was supposed to have remarked (his enemies claimed), "As a child, I used to swear to myself that I would be a member of the Academy. It is the only vow I have ever kept." *The Memoirs of Chancellor Pasquier*, p. 282, fn. 9.

21 Messengers were widely used before the telephone.

22 The bell that summoned students and teachers to class had been brought from Saint Catherine's convent, where the school had been briefly located under Haüy. It was installed, along with a clock also from the former convent, on the roof of the building on rue Saint-Victor. Guillié, *Rapport* 1820, p. 7.

23 Roblin 1951, p. 72.

BRAILLE BANNED

1 Since no one knew how to emboss pages of braille, metal casts of entire pages of complete braille cells were made. Repeaters and students then used burins to scrape unneeded dots from each cell. The paper pages were embossed from these metal sheets.

2 Dufau started his career at the school as a geography teacher.

3 E. Guilbeau, *Histoire de l'institution nationale des jeunes aveugles*, 1907, p. 81. Quoted in Weygand 2003, p. 322. Guilbeau became a student at the Institution in 1858, and later taught history and geography.

4 Dufau was well aware that Alexis de Noailles, a trustee of the Institution and well-known royalist with counter-revolutionary views, strongly supported Pignier. See *The Memoirs of Chancellor Pasquier*, 1968, p. 130.

5 Roblin 1951, p. 21.

6 Ibid., p. 86.

7 "Education of the Blind" [written anonymously by Samuel Gridley Howe], *North American Review*, 1833, p. 19. Howe's views on Catholicism may have colored his judgments. Unaware of its insulting tone, he once said of Abbé Charles Carton, with whom he and his wife, Julia Ward Howe, spent a delightful couple of days in 1843, "although a good Catholic, he is a very intelligent and high-minded man." Letter to Charles Sumner, August 27, 1843.

8 Ibid., pp. 27-28.

9 Ibid., p. 28.

10 Weygand 2003, p. 336.

11 The *Pater Noster* (1837) was formatted in two columns, with Latin, French, Italian, Spanish, German, or English in braille in one column, and the embossed print version in the adjacent column. Henri 1952, p. 76.

12 The braille edition, embossed in 1837, was transcribed from the 10th print edition of the book, which implies that it had enjoyed a wide readership. Henri 1952, p. 72.

13 Howe 1833, p. 19.

14 Ramon de la Sagra, *Cinco Meses en los Estados-Unidos*, 1836, pp. 30, 366-368. Dufau mentions this research in the 1850 edition of *Des aveugles*, pp. 114-115. I would like to thank Pedro Zurita, formerly of O.N.C.E., Madrid, and Evelio Montes, research librarian at O.N.C.E., for tracking down de la Sagra's book and sending me copies of the relevant pages.

15 Roblin 1951, p. 96.

16 Ibid., p. 91.

17 Ibid., p. 99.

18 Ibid., p. 90.

19 Henri 1952, pp. 73-74 strongly doubts that braille could have been written in secret because it makes a distinctive noise and requires special materials. Production of braille documents evidently began soon after the inauguration ceremony. Henri, who was also blind, reports that a brailled edition of *Way of the Cross* has a perfectly clear notation on it, "Transcribed by J-P Lamirault, student at the Royal Institution, 1844."

20 Roblin 1951, p. 91.

21 Ibid., pp. 96-97.

22 Henri 1952, p. 73.

23 For a brief introduction to Klein see, "Johann Wilhelm Klein: A Portrait" in *Berthold Lowenfeld on Blindness and Blind People*, AFB, 1981, pp. 144-147. I wish to thank Susi Alteneder of the Vienna Institute for the Blind (BBI), Vienna, for allowing me to examine this decapoint letter.

24 Ibid., p. 146.

25 Roblin 1951, p. 88.

26 Sizeranne, *Guadet et les aveugles*, 1885, p. 9.

27 Roblin 1951, p. 100.

28 Ibid., pp. 100-101.

29 Louis was not completely in the shade. In 1839, his students asked that he receive the Cross of Honor (*Croix d'Honneur*). Roblin 1952, p. 84. Henri 1952, p. 120 suggests that this request came at a later date. Pierre-Armand Dufau, on the other hand, received the *Legion d'Honneur* in 1849.

30 P. A. Dufau, *Des aveugles*, 1850, pp. 123-124.

31 Ibid., p. 102.

32 Letters were not sent in envelopes, but were folded up and sealed with wax; the address was written in a blank space on the outside.

33 In Auvergne.

34 Translated by Ernest Alfred Vizetelly, 1913, pp. 11 and 12.

35 Roblin 1951, p. 108.

GLOBAL BRAILLE

1 Sir Francis Bond Head, 1793-1875, traveler, essayist, and biographer.

2 Vol. 2, pp. 504-505.

3 Bruno Liesen, "Le braille: origine, reception et diffusion" in *Voir barré*, No. 23, December 2001, p. 23.

4 Weygand 2003, p. 341.

5 Dr. Simon Pollack, founder of the Missouri School, happened to be in France just after braille was officially adopted in 1854, and brought details of the code back with him.

6 Armitage 1871, pp. 15-16.

7 Brazil's connection with braille dates to 1854, when the Emperor of Brazil paid, out of his own pocket, for casting a new type font to be used at the Paris Institution to braille a book on reading [braille] in Portuguese. Henri 1952, p. 75.

8 This was in the mistaken belief that cells with the least number of dots were the easiest to read. It *was* easier to write, using a slate and stylus, because fewer dots had to be impressed. It did not save space in a book because the same number of cells was required.

9 Universal Congress for the amelioration of the condition of the blind and deafblind.

10 Henri 1952, p. 81.

11 Ibid., p. 127, fn. 2. The word "braille" (no initial capital letter) is generally used to designate the code, while "Braille" (with a capital letter) refers to Louis Braille, the man.

12 Invented by William Moon, a blind man, this embossed type used simplified shapes of print letters and a few other shapes easily identified by the fingertips. It continued to be produced in the UK for most of the 20th century. The *Matilda Ziegler Magazine for the Blind* published a Moon Type edition from 1934 through 1965.

13 Henri 1951, pp. 78-80.

14 When the *Matilda Ziegler Magazine for the Blind* began production in 1907, it had to manufacture both braille and New York Point editions. NYP was the more popular, with 4,500 copies embossed, compared with 2,000 [American] braille. The NYP edition was discontinued in 1963.

15 Braille contractions are used to save space, with one letter sometimes standing for a word. Just a few cells are used for such common suffixes as "ing" and "tion." This principle is familiar to anyone who uses a cell phone for text messaging, where, for example, "btw" stands for "by the way," "ttyl" means, "talk to you later," and "gal" stands for "get a life."

16 Quoted in C. Michael Mellor, "Making a Point" [*Faisons le point*] in *Second International Conference on the Blind in History*, 1998 [in French and English], p. 34.

17 Henri 1951, p. 83.

18 Sir Clutha Mackenzie, *World Braille Usage*, 1954, p. 23.

19 William B. Wait, *New Aspects of the Uniform Type Folly*, 1916.

20 Robert B. Irwin, *The War of the Dots*, American Foundation for the Blind, 1955.

21 Quoted in Koestler, *The Unseen Minority*, p. 97.

22 Henri 1952, p. 89.

23 Two individuals who have advanced the cause of braille are Kim Charlson, current chair of The Braille Authority of North America (BANA), and director of the Perkins Braille & Talking Book Library in Watertown, Massashusetts; and Joe Sullivan, president of Duxbury Systems in Westford, Massachusetts, and the original developer of a braille translation software that now handles over 50 languages, math, and braille graphics. Both assisted me with this explanation of current developments in the braille code.

24 *Braille Into the Next Millennium*, 2000, p. 66.

25 This is achieved by slightly offsetting the position of the cells so that dots on one side do not flatten those embossed on the other side. Both sides are embossed simultaneously.

26 Mackenzie 1954, p. 27.

27 United Nations Educational, Scientific and Cultural Organization. Sir Clutha Mackenzie, author of *World Braille Usage: A Survey of Efforts towards Uniformity of Braille Notation*, was braille consultant to UNESCO and chairman of the World Braille Council, which was founded by UNESCO in 1919.

Bibliography

Armitage, T.R. *The Education and Employment of the Blind.* London, 1871.

Artman, W. and L.V. Hall. *Beauties and Achievements of the Blind.* Rochester, NY, 1874.

Bickel, Lennard. *Triumph over Darkness.* Allen & Unwin Australia, 1988.

Blum, Christpher Olaf (ed). *Critics of the Enlightenment.* ISI Books, 2004.

Briggs, Asa. *Victorian Things.* Sutton, 2003.

Bullock, Alan. *The Humanist Tradition in the West.* Norton, 1985.

Chaptal, Antoine. *Mes souvenirs/Sur Napoléon.* Paris, 1893.

Coltat, Hippolyte. "Notice biographique sur L. Braille." In *Inauguration du buste de Louis Braille.* Paris, 1853.

Désormeaux, Jean (ed). *Deuxième conférence internationale sur les aveugles dans l'histoire et l'histoire des aveugles/Second International Conference on the Blind in History and the History of the Blind.* Association Valentin Haüy, 1998.

Dixon, Judith M. (ed). *Braille Into the Next Millennium.* National Library Service for the Blind and Physically Handicapped and Friends of Libraries for Blind and Physically Handicapped Individuals in North America. Washington, D.C., 2000.

Dufau, Pierre-Armand. *Des aveugles.* Paris, 1850.

Freedman, Russell. *Out of Darkness.* Clarion Books, 1997.

Garrioch, David. *The Making of Revolutionary Paris.* U. California Press, 2002.

Gay, Peter. *The Enlightenment: An Interpretation,* 2 vols. Knopf, 1966-1969.

Guillié, Sébastien. *Essai sur l'instruction des aveugles.* Paris, 1817, 1819.

——————. *Rapport fait à son excellence le ministre, secrétaire d'état au département de l'intérieur.* Paris, 1818, 1820.

Haüy, Valentin. *Essai sur l'éducation des aveugles.* Paris, 1786.

Henri, Pierre. *La vie et oeuvre de Louis Braille.* Groupement des intellectuels aveugles ou amblyopes, 1952.

——————. *La vie et œuvre de Valentin Haüy.* Presses universitaires de France, 1984.

Himmelfarb, Gertrude. *The Roads to Modernity.* Knopf, 2004.

Husson, Thérèse-Adèle. *Reflections.* [Translated and with commentary by Catherine J. Kudlick and Zina Weygand.] NYU Press, 2001.

Irwin, Robert B. "The War of the Dots." In *As I Saw It.* American Foundation for the Blind, 1955.

Koestler, Frances A. *The Unseen Minority.* McKay, 1976. Paperback, American Foundation for the Blind, 2004.

Krolick, Bettye. *How to Read Braille Music: An Introduction.* 2nd Ed. Opus Technologies, 1998.

Kudlick, Catherine J, and Zina Weygand, see Husson.

Lawhorn, Geraldine. *On Different Roads.* Vantage, 1991.

Lorimer, Pamela. *Reading by Touch.* National Federation of the Blind, 2000.

Lowenfeld, Berthold. *Berthold Lowenfeld on Blindness and Blind People.* American Foundation for the Blind, 1981.

Mackenzie, Sir Clutha. *World Braille Usage.* UNESCO, 1954.

Magee, Martin and Martin Milligan. *On Blindness.* Oxford University Press, 1995.

Montaigne, Michel de. *The Complete Essays.* [Translated by M.A. Screech.] Allen Lane/Penguin, 1991.

Pasquier, Etienne. *The Memoirs of Chancellor Pasquier.* [Translated by Douglas Garman.] Fairleigh Dickinson UP, 1968.

Pignier, Alexandre François-René. *Notices Biographiques sur trois professeurs.* Paris, 1859.

Roblin, Jean. *Les doigts qui lisent.* Regain, 1951. A translation of this book, abridged, *The Reading Fingers,* was published by AFB in 1952.

Robyn, Henry. *To the Trustees, Principals, and Teachers of Blind Asylums.* Saint Louis, 1866.

Schama, Simon. *Citizens.* Vintage, 1989.
Shearing, George with Shipton, Alyn. *Lullaby of Birdland.* The Continuum International Publishing Group, 2004.

Taesch, Richard & William McCann. *Who's Afraid of Braille Music???* Dancing Dots Braille Music Technology, 2003.
Tomlinson, Charles (ed.). *Cyclopedia of Useful Arts.* London, 1854.

Van Landeghem, (Mrs.) Hippolyte. *The Advantages of Social Education for the Blind.* London, 1865.
Vaughan, Ernest. *Notice historique sur les Quinze-Vingts.* Paris, 1909.

Weiner, Dora B. *The Citizen-Patient.* Johns Hopkins University Press, 1993.
Weygand, Zina. *Vivre sans voir.* Créaphis, 2003.
Wilson, Arthur M. *Diderot.* Oxford University Press, 1972.
Wilson, James. *Biography of the Blind.* Library of Congress, 1995. [From original editions, 1821-38.]
Woloch, Isser. *Napoleon and His Collaborators.* Norton, 2001.

Zola, Emile. *Lourdes.* [Translated by E. A. Vizetelly.] Chatto & Windus, 1913.

Index

Page numbers in italics denote illustrations.